# Ogham and Coelbren
## Mystic Signs and Symbols of the Celtic Druids

### Nigel Pennick

www.capallbann.co.uk

# Ogham and Coelbren

©2000 Nigel Pennick

ISBN 186163 102 2

**ALL RIGHTS RESERVED**

No part of this publication may be reproduced, stored in a retrieval system or transmitted in any form or by any means, electronic, mechanical, photocopying, scanning, recording or otherwise without the prior written permission of the author and the publisher.

Cover design by Paul Mason
Cover and internal illustration by Nigel Pennick

Published by:

Capall Bann Publishing
Freshfields
Chieveley
Berks
RG20 8TF

*Mider, guardian of the gateway to the Otherworld. The Bardo-Druldic alphabets are a inner gateways to the same realms.*

# Thanks and Credits

I wish to thank the following people and institutions for various assistance or information that was forthcoming at certain times in the genesis and preparation of *Ogham and Coelbren*: Helen Field, Ernst Hug, Nigel Jackson, K. Frank Jensen, Prudence Jones, Barbara Meyer, the late Colin Murray, Rosemarie Kirschmann; Seán Pennick, Cambridge University Library; Welsh Folk Museum, St Fagan's; National Museum of Antiquities, Dublin; British Museum, London; the Pitt-Rivers Museum, Oxford; Württembergisches Landesmuseum, Stuttgart; and the Narrenschopf Bad Dürrheim.

# Contents

| | | |
|---|---|---|
| Foreword | | 1 |
| Chapter 1 | The Irish Tree 'Alphabet' | 5 |
| Chapter 2 | Meanings of the Ogham Feadha | 27 |
| Chapter 3 | Ogham Cryptography, Gall Ogham and the Gaelic Alphabet | 68 |
| Chapter 4 | Deities of the Sacred Forest | 82 |
| Chapter 5 | Celtic Tree-Lore of Birch, Thorn and Oak | 108 |
| Chapter 6 | Welsh Bardic Scripts | 124 |
| Appendices | List of Contents | 147 |
| Appendix 1 | Glossary of Terms | 149 |
| Appendix 2 | | 157 |
| Appendix 3 | Classification of Celtic Tree Types | 159 |
| Appendix 4 | | 161 |
| Appendix 5 | The Tree-Months | 162 |
| Appendix 6 | The Oghams and The New Celtic Oracle | 163 |
| Appendix 7 | The Thirteen Precious Things of the Island of Britain | 165 |
| Appendix 8 | Time and Space in the Welsh Tradition | 167 |
| Appendix 9 | Bardo-Druidic Chronology | 169 |
| Appendix 10 | Welsh Traditional Astronomy: The Thirty-Seven Constellations | 171 |
| Appendix 11 | The Bardic Hierarchy | 174 |
| Bibliography | | 175 |

i

# Foreword

My earlier publications on the Celtic Bardo-Druidic 'alphabets' appeared in 1978 and 1988. *Ogham and Coelbren* is a complete revision that adds to and supersedes my previous work on these systems, being a full exposition of both the Irish and Welsh Bardo-Druidic 'alphabets' and their associated lore. The Ogham lore described here is based upon the extant recorded sources, especially the *Book of Ballymote*, the *Auraicept na nÉces*, ancient Irish law and Welsh Bardic writings collected together in the nineteenth century. From these ancient writings, it is clear that there is an underlying unity in spirit in the Bardo-Druidry of Great Britain and Ireland. Vernacular traditions and spiritual practices from all of the Celtic lands reinforce this essential cultural unity.

According to ancient writings from both Ireland and Wales, the Bardo-Druidic tradition comes out of the wild wood, both in the sense of the symbolism of individual trees, and the woodlands they comprise. Trees are a Celtic metaphor of human consciousness, overtly so in the Welsh language. The trees of the natural, uncut forest parallel the inner, tameless part of the human soul: they are deep symbols of natural wildness.

Such wildness should never be considered to be a state of being out of control. Rather it represents innate naturalness that exists in balanced harmony with natural principles. Eternal, elemental powers reside in the forest, and those who enter them on a quest may encounter them. When we return to the wild occasionally, then the wildwood gives us the possibility of deep psychic transformation. In the wildwood,

1. The Celtic spiritual landscape is present at all levels of being.

we can re-establish our conscious link with our inner instincts by contacting the 'Green Man' or 'Wild Woman' within all of us.

Once we are supported by the elemental powers of the wood, we can rediscover forgotten things that contemporary civilization often ignores. Ceremonies of 'Maying' and 'Greenwood Marriages' in the woods are a means of doing this. But we can only do so if the untouched wildwood still exists on both the outer and the inner levels. Once it has been destroyed, then the wild part of the human soul is no longer accessible. Reintegration is no longer possible, and the wasteland comes apace. Through the use of Ogham and Coelbren, the inner trees of the Bardo-Druidic system can be a significant means of reconnecting us with the outer Nature of which we are all part.

Nigel Campbell Pennick
Bar Hill,
Mys Myri 25, 2479 EP (1999 CE).

2. Ogham standing stone from County Kerry, with Pagan and Christian symbols.

# Chapter 1
# The Irish Tree 'Alphabet'

## The Origin and A Brief Overview of Ogham

The form of writing known as Ogham was used in historic times in Ireland and the western parts of ancient Britain. Its precise age is uncertain, though some have claimed that is was in existence as early as 2200 BCE. This dating depends upon the interpretation of marks on some small slabs of chalk discovered during excavations at Windmill Hill in southern England. Alexander Keiller found seventeen of them, and the marks were interpreted as Ogham. Most academics do not accept that Ogham existed so early. According to Professor Brendan O'Hehir of the University of Berkeley, California, the earliest dateable Ogham is from around the second century CE. Also, it is certain that all of the definite Ogham inscriptions are Irish or with Irish connections. Those who hold that the Windmill Hill stones are Ogham must explain the two thousand year gap in use and also the change of location from Great Britain to Ireland.

Early modern researchers into Ogham at first claimed that it was derived from Greek sources, even Hellennic semaphore that used blazing torches, but, more recently, the Latin (Roman) alphabet has been favoured as its base. Several hundred ancient Ogham inscriptions are known to exist. They have been found on rock faces, standing stones, Celtic crosses, portable artifacts and in manuscripts. In the 1940s, R.A.S. Macalister published a collection of all known Ogham inscriptions on stone from the British Isles. There were 385 in all. Most of them (320) are in Ireland, of which 130 are in County Kerry (60 are from the Dingle Peninsula alone); Cork 84; Waterford 48; and the rest scattered through Leinster and the eastern seaboard. The Barony of Corco Duibne, where Ogham stones are most numerous, is a kind of archaic originplace where, according to legendary history, all manner of significant changes were first introduced to Ireland.

Most of the other ancient Ogham stones are in places where Irish invasions and colonization took place: the Isle of Man, Scotland, Wales and the former Dumnonia (Cornwall and Devon). Between the third and sixth centuries CE, there were continued invasions of Great Britain from Ireland. Irish invasions of western Britain were extensive. They involved relatively short occupations of parts of (what is now) Wales and Cornwall, and a permanent conquest of Caledonia (north Britain) by the Scots from the north of Ireland.

The Irish text, *The Expulsion of the Déssi*, tells how, around the year 265 CE, accompanied by his family and followers, Eochaid, son of Artchorp, invaded the territory of Demed (Dyfed, Wales). There, "his sons and grandsons died". From them came 'the Race of Crimthann'. Cormac's ninth century CE Glossary also mentions Irish incursions into Great Britain: "At that time. The power of the Gaels [Irish] was great over the Britons. They had divided Alba [Scotland] into estates among themselves... and the Gaels used to live to the east of the sea no less than in Scotia [Ireland]...their dwellings and their royal castles were built there....every tribe had property on the east [Great Britain] equal to that on the west [Ireland], and they continued in power for a long time, even after the coming of St Patrick".

In the sixth century, the dynasty of the ethnic British (Welsh), Brythonic-speaking Cunedda ruled north Wales, whilst the south was ruled by Goidelic-speaking ethnic Irish. The boundary lay roughly along a line between the Dee and the Teifi rivers. The Ogham stones in Wales are certainly the product of these Irish colonies. Around fifty have been noted. Most are inscribed with Christian texts in Latin as well as Irish Ogham. By the style of the accompanying Roman letters, most date from the fifth and sixth centuries CE, mostly before the year 550.

The Ogham stones are Irish memorials, inscribed with a formula: the name of the dead person is always given in its genitive form, inferring "the grave of", or "the stone of". Some stones give a single name, whilst others record the deceased's patrilinearity. A stone from Nevern in Pembrokeshire is typical, reading: *Maglicunas Maqi Clutari*, "the stone (or grave) of Maglicu Mac [son of] Clutarius". Another, at Brynkir in Caernarvonshire, carries only a single name, Icorigas, meaning "the stone (or grave) of Icorix". Some Ogham inscriptions have, instead of *Maqi*, 'son of', *Avi*, 'grandson' or 'descendent of', or *Ingenia*, 'daughter of'.

Because Ogham was an Irish form of writing, it died out in Wales when most ethnic Irish were exterminated and the survivors expelled during the Welsh resurgence of the seventh century. For many years, one of the landmarks for sailors on the Irish Sea was a vast cairn of Irish skulls heaped up on a headland at Holyhead in Anglesey. In Caledonia, the Irish conquest was permanent. The indigenous Picts were largely exterminated, and the survivors absorbed, whilst the British (Welsh) were expelled from Strathclyde and Scotland came into being.

Although most ancient surviving inscriptions are memorials, from medieval and later texts, we know that the Ogham 'alphabet' also had a symbolic aspect. When Christian missionaries introduced the Roman alphabet to Ireland, and, later, Scandinavian settlers brought the Runes, these scripts, and not Ogham were preferred for memorials. In Ireland and western Britain, there are monuments upon which both Ogham and Roman letters co-exist. By the end of the sixth century, Ogham had gone out of use on public monuments. However, by the ninth century, craftsmen had begun to use *Ogham Feadha* ('characters').

Some of the Ogham stones on the Isle of Man, Scotland and Shetland are later than those in the rest of Britain, dating from the tenth to the twelfth centuries. Their inscriptions are known among Oghamists as *Scholastic Oghams* which are also found on metal artifacts from monasteries and the courts of kings and lords. This type of Ogham differs from the earlier form because the *Feadha* are cut across an engraved line, not the *Arris* (edge) of the stone (see Chapter 2).

*Scholastic Oghams* are in the style of manuscript Ogham texts. The only inscriptions from mainland Europe that have any reason to be called Ogham date from this time, when Irish monks travelled central Europe founding monasteries following the Celtic Christian rule. *Scholastic Oghams* are defined as dating between the ninth and seventeenth century. Contemporary Oghams are a continuation of the 'scholastic' tradition by way of manuscripts and the researches of antiquaries of the eighteenth and nineteenth centuries.

In addition to their use by 'scholars', Oghams were part of the vernacular learning of the 'Plain People of Ireland', too. History provides sporadic instances, for example, in the nineteenth century, a man surnamed Collins was brought before a magistrate in County Cork because he had not painted his name on his cart, as required by law. He was able to explain that his name was on the cart - written in Ogham - and was acquitted. The nineteenth century antiquary John Windle carried a stick inscribed with Ogham. He, and the parish priest of Blarney, the Reverend Matthew Horgan, were avid preservers of Ogham learning.

An Irish vernacular rhyme mentioned by Mac Curtin in 1732 and recorded (in English) by collectors in the nineteenth century began:

"For B one stroke at your right hand,
And L doth always two demand;
For F draw three; for S make four;
When you want N, you add one more......"

This country rhyme contains the description of all of the Ogham Feadha, and how they are written. It was the key by which the antiquaries, first of all the Right Reverend Bishop Graves, were able to decipher ancient Ogham inscriptions.

In the middle of the nineteenth century, 'Celtic Revival' artifacts became popular among the ruling class in Ireland and Britain. They included the *Clarendon Shawl Brooch* otherwise called *The Ogham Pin.* Made by the jewellers Waterhouse and Company from 1849 onwards, this was a replica of the 'Ballyspellan Brooch', a medieval Celtic artifact with scholastic Ogham inscriptions on the reverse side. Waterhouse offered these brooches either in gold with Irish pearls, silver, or silver gilt inlaid with Bog Oak, copies of this brooch brought Ogham to public attention for the first time since early medieval times.

During the twentieth century, the poet Robert Graves further popularized Ogham through his book *The White Goddess* (1947), where he interpreted ancient Celtic poetry in the light of the 'Tree Alphabet'. This gave an impetus to the esoteric study of Ogham which was further refined in the 1970s in England by Colin Murray in his Druidic organization called *The Golden Section Order.* Murray was the first person to put Ogham into the form of divination cards. Since then, Ogham has become an integral part of the teachings of Celtic spirituality.

3. The Ballyspellan Brooch, front and back with scholastic Ogham inscriptions.

This brief history of Ogham demonstrates that it has developed over time from carvings on the edges of standing stones to bookish and metal forms and finally divination cards. The interpretation of the meanings of the individual *Feadha* have also varied and developed through their history. Apart from their phonetic meanings, we do not know what esoteric significance the earliest Ogham had. Later manuscripts, especially *The Book of Ballymote* (see below), give us full descriptions of numerous esoteric correspondences, which may or may not have existed earlier. Other commentaries exist in the text called *Uraicecht na n Eiges* or *Auraicept na nÉces* (variously translated as *The Hearings of the Scholars*, *The Precepts of the Poets*, or *The Scholars' Primer*). This tells how the autonomous colleges of Druidry and Bardism, and also independent Bards, developed individual and variant systems of correspondences for the Ogham *Feadha*. These, in turn, are developed, reinterpreted and sometimes contradicted by later texts.

More recently, the twentieth century commentators added their own interpretations, in line with modern scholar-ship: in some cases modifying and changing earlier ascriptions. All of these forms attest to the dynamic continuous development of Ogham for the best part of two millennia, and as with all dynamic systems, there has never been a fixed point in history that states "this is definitive". However, Ogham does have a recognizable 'spirit', which, although it is not a simple thing to define it precisely, has determined the past history and the present uses of the 'Celtic Tree Alphabet'.

### Legendary Origins: Ogma Grian Aineach

The legendary Irish warrior champion Ogma Grian Aineach, 'the sun-countenanced' is described in the Tain Bó Cúalnge (The Cattle-Raid of Cooley) as a son of the father (god) known as The Dagda. Ruling from the Sídhe of Airceltrai, Ogma was skilled in the use of words, and known consequently by the

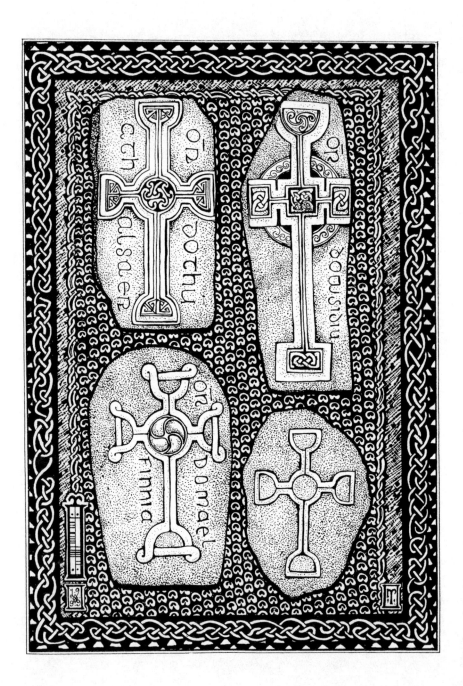

name of 'Ogma Cermait', 'the honey-mouthed'. However, according to *The Book of Ballymote*, Ogma was the son of Elathan, and brother of Breass MacElathan, the Ard Rí (High King) of all Ireland. Ogma Grian Aineach MacElathan bears a forename similar to that of a Gaulish god. The Roman author Lucian, in his *dialogue* on Hercules mentions Ogmios as the Celtic equivalent to the Graeco-Roman demi-god. He describes an image he saw in Gaul, that showed Ogmios as a dark-skinned old man clad in a lion's skin, and carrying a club and a bow. Chains of amber and gold emanated from the tip of his tongue to bind the ears of captives, who followed him willingly.

Lucian was told that Ogmios personified the power of eloquence and wisdom, which only develops fully in old age. A god called Ogmios is also known from Bregenz, an old Celtic centre in the Vorarlberg of Austria. There, he appears with the underworldly deities Dis Pater and Aeracura, and is assumed to be a psychopomp or guide of the dead in the underworld like they are. The golden chains described by Lucian appear as golden rays in a Romano-British image of Ogmios, echoing the Irish 'sun-countenanced' epithet of Ogma. Also a fragment of pottery found at Rutupiae (Richborough) depicts a god with rays coming from the head and a whip in his hand, with the inscription *Ogmia*.

According to the Tract on Ogham in the *Book of Ballymote* (Folios 308-314), Ogma, the epitome of eloquence and wisdom, was the legendary inventor of the Ogham alphabet. Irish texts depict Ogma as a champion warrior who is skilled in languages to the point of originating a dialect and an 'alphabet'.

---

*Opposite: 4.Early medieval Irish mentorial slabs with Gaeilge alphabet inscriptions, Clockwise from top left: stone of the smith Tuathall Saer at Clonmacnois, County Offaly; stone of Algidu, Durrow, Co, Offaly uninscribed cross-slab, Clonmacnois; slab dedicated to Mael Finnia, Clonmacnois.*

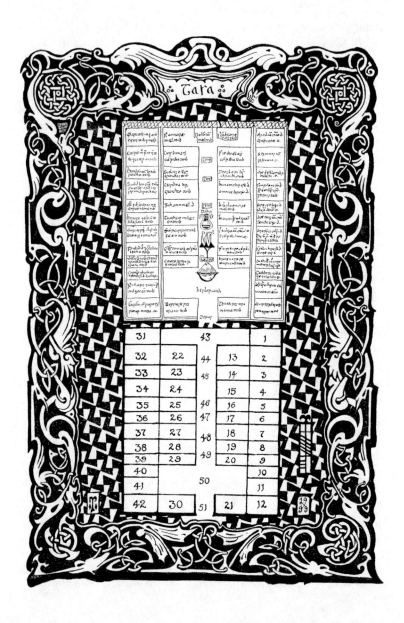

The *Auricept na nÉces* recounts how Ogma employed a twig of Birch to carve the first Oghams. It carried a message to Lug MacEthlenn, telling him that his wife would be abducted seven times into the Otherworld "unless the Birch guard her". The Ogham carving consisted of seven single strokes to the left of the *droim* (centre line, see Chapter 2, *Ogham Terminology*), seven Bs. This story appears to be an origin-myth to explain the primacy of the Birch in the Oghams. According to the *Book of Ballymote*, Ogma's intention in inventing Ogham was as a secret cipher, "for signs of secret speech only known to the learned, and designed to be kept from the vulgar and poor of the nation". Corroborating this use are the one hundred and fifty different varieties of Ogham recorded in the *Book of Ballymote*.

Cormac, in his ninth century CE *Glossary* recounts how the Oghams were used by the early Pagan Irish before the time of

---

*Opposite: 5. Layout of the great hall of the High Kings of Ir-eland at Tars according to The Yellow Book of Lucan showing ritual seating positions of the classes of ancient Irish society (south at the top): 1 Charioteers and Stewards; 2 Deerstalkers; 3 Airs Foraill (first-grade nobility); 4 High King and Queen; Aire Ard (3rd grade nobility) and Cli (3rd grade poets); 6 Aire Tusi (2nd grade nobility) and Historians; 7 Aire Desa 14th grade nobility and Dos (5th grade poets); 13 Fochloc (6th grade poets); 9 Cooks 10 Fortress engineers; 11 Champions and Cane (4th grade poets); 12 Sappers 13 Board-game players; 14 Spencers; 15 Braziers; 16 Physicians; 17 Pilots; 18 Merchants; 19 Jesters; 20 Buffoons; 21 King's Fools; 22 Flute-players; 23 Schoolteachers; 24 Goldsmiths; 25 Smiths; 26 Shield-makers; 27 Chariot-wrights; 28 Conjurors; 29 Satirists; 30 Doorkeepers; 3l Horsemen; 32 Harpers and Drummers; 33 Judges; 34 Doctors of Letters and their nominated successors; 35 Chief Poets and Anrwith (2nd grade poets) 36 Hospitallers; 37 Master Wrights and their successors; 38 Soothsayers and Druids; 3! Bui lders and Wr i gh t s; 40 Pipers and Trumpeters; 41 Engravers; 42 Cordwainers; 43 Servants; 44, 45, 46 Hearths; 47 Cauldron; 48 Candlestick; 49 Lantern; 50 Common Hall; 51 Door.*

St Patrick and his followers. He tells of the *Mete-wand* or measuring rod used to measure bodies for burials. On them were written in Ogham "whatever was hateful or detestable relating to them, and left it in the graveyard". In Chapter xiv of his English-Irish dictionary of 1732, MacCurtin wrote: "of the ancient character called *Ogam* and of the abbreviations called *Nodaighe*.....Irish antiquaries preserved this *Ogam* as a piece of the greatest value in all antiquity, and it was penal for anyone to study or use it but one of the sworn antiquaries. In those characters the antiquaries wrote the evil acts of their monarchs and great personages, male and female, so that it may not be known to the vulgar or common multitude, only to the learned; and for the better understanding of these characters it is necessary to get and keep by heart certain verses in the Irish language."

A parallel to this keeping of secret records of 'evil acts' is practised in south Germany to this day by certain masked participants in the Schwäbish-Allemannisch Fasnacht ceremonies around Shrovetide. Called *Schandtle*, they carry small books recording such deeds, and whisper them, in disguised voices to the individuals concerned. The historic connection with earlier times is uncertain, but the function of Bards, Jesters and Fools often overlaps in traditional society.

## Historical Records of Ogham

The oldest Irish historical stories contain many references to the Ogham alphabet, often as sepulchral memorials. In the *Leabhar na hUidhré*, for example, the grave of the third century CE king Fothadh Airgtheach is said to have had *Fothad Airgthech ind ro*, 'Fothadh Airgthech here' inscribed in Oghams. The story of Deirdre tells of her joint tomb with Naisi: "Their stone was raised over their monument, their Ogham names were written, and their ceremony of lamentation was performed". In a poem recorded in *The Book of Leinster*, we are told of "Ogham on the stone, the stone over the monument...". Recording a battle fought in the third century CE, we are told:

> "That Ogham which is on the stone
> Around which many were slain;
> If Finn of the many battles lived,
> Long would the Ogham be remembered".

From texts and from extant memorials in Ireland and Wales, it appears that the Oghams carved on stone monuments usually contained only the names of those commemorated. But, as the *Auraicept na néces* records, Oghams carved on wood could have a magical or secret function. The *Leabhar na hUidhré*, a manuscript dating from 1106, contains the story of the *Tain Bó Cúalnge* (often Anglicized as *The Cattle-Raid of Cooley*). In it, the hero Cuchulaínn cuts Oghams on willow withies that he bends into a hoop. These are interpreted by Fergus in the army of Queen Medb. The story of the exile of the sons of Duil Dermait tells how Cuchulaínn inscribes Oghams on a spear, giving it talismanic powers. The *Book of Leinster* also tells of the exile of Corc, who was driven out by his father, Lughaidh, king of Munster. Arriving in Caledonia, Corc was recognized by Gruibné, Bard of King Feradach. Examining Corc's shield, the Bard discovered an Ogham inscription on it, the ominous meaning of which Corc was ignorant.

In addition to inscriptions upon stone, the ancient Irish reckoned four other ways of writing the Oghams. They are *Tamlorga Filidh*, 'Staves of the Poets'; *Tabhall Lorga*, 'Tablet Staves'; *Fleasc Filidh*, 'The Wand of the Poet'; and *Taibhli Fileadh*, 'Tables of the Poets'. The exact form of the *Taibhli Fileadh* is unknown. However, descriptions of them seem to liken them to certain ancient runic calendars known from Scandinavia. These are in the form of a wooden fan, which, when closed, looked something live a baton or staff. The traditional Irish law-code known as the Brehon Laws gives the privilege or 'badge of office' of a Bard as a *Tabhall-Lorg* ('Tablet-Staff').

The story of Bailé MacBuain, 'The Sweet Spoken', the favourite lover of Aillinn, tells how some of them came into being. At the place where they were buried, an Apple and a Yew tree grew on their graves (Q and I in Ogham). After seven years, the Bards of Ulster cut down the Yew that grew over Bailé, and made a *Tabhall Fileadh* ('Poets' Tablet') from it. On the tablet, they wrote "the visions, and marriages, and lovers, and the courtships of Ulster".

They also cut down the Apple of Aillinn, and on the tablet made from its wood, they inscribed the visions, marriages, lovers and courtships of Leinster. These tablets finally ceased to be usable in the time of King Art, son of Conn of the Hundred Battles (166 CE). At the feast of Samhain, as was customary, the Bards and professors of all of the arts gathered together at the king's court, to read from their tablets. The tablets of Bailé and Aillinn were given to Art, but, as he was reading them, suddenly they closed together, and could never again be separated.

## Ogham in the Book of Ballymote

The most important source of Ogham is the *The Book of Ballymote*, a major text written at Ballymote in the county of Sligo in the house of Tomaltagh Og MacDonough, Lord of Corann. It dates from the time that Tourlough Og, the son of Hugh O'Conor, was king of Connacht. Charles O'Conor of Belanagar later inserted the date 1391 (on *Folio* 62b). The Book of Ballymote is composed of 252 leaves of vellum in the large folio format ($10^{1}/_{2}$ by $13^{1}/_{2}$ inches: 26.67 x 34.29 cm). Its pages were transcribed by several hands, mainly by Solomon O'Droma and Manus O'Duigenann. The text is a compilation of various material from older manuscripts. It commences with a version of the *Lebor Gabála Erenn* (*The Book of Invasions of Ireland*).

Following this are several chronologies and historical episodes in poetry and prose. After them come the genealogies of Irish saints and the notable tribes and families of the Milesian Race; the acts of various kings and other episodes from Irish mythological history. There is a treatise on ancient Irish grammar and prosody, *Uraicecht na néiges*, ascribed to Fercetne, the chief Fili (Bard) of the King of Ulster, Conor MacNessa, and enlarged around 628 CE by Cennfaeladh, son of Ailill. Next, and most importantly for our purposes, there is an illustrated treatise on the Ogham alphabets of the ancient Irish. The book ends with a text on the adventures of Aeneas after the fall of Troy.

In the section headed *Oghaim na nGadhel* (*The Irish Oghams*), the *Book of Ballymote* gives the following explanation in the traditional catechismal question-and-answer form:

"From whence, what time, and what person, and from what cause, did the Ogham spring?

The place is Hibernia's Isle, which we Scots inhabit; in the time of Breas, the son of Elathan, then king of all Ireland. The person was Ogma, the son of Elathan, the son of Dealbadh, brother to Breas, for Breas, Ogma and Dealbadh were three sons of Elathan, who was the son of Dealbath. Ogma, being a man much skilled in dialects and in poetry, it was he who invented the Ogham, its object being for signs of secret speech only known to the learned, and designed to be kept from the vulgar and poor of the nation.

Where were the names and figures of the Ogham found? Who were the mother and the father of the Ogham? What was the first name written in Ogham characters? What tree was it written in? Why was it written? What was written? And from whom came the art of numbering and forming books regularly in Ogham?.

It is called Ogham from Ogma, the inventor. The derivation is *Oghaim*, from *Ghuaim*, that is, the *guaim*, or wisdom through which the Bards were enabled to compose [equivalent to the Welsh *Awen* - N.P.]; for by its branches the Irish Bards sounded their verses.The father of Ogham was Ogma, and the mother of Ogham was the hand or knife of Ogma. *Soim* was the first thing written in Ogham. It was written in a Birch, and given to Lug, the son of Etlem, with an explanation multiplying branches, which ran as from the roots, namely: seven slips in one sheath slip thus, and gave them folded, called male and female, another name, man or woman, of the Birch; for of the Birch they first wrote Oghams.

How many and what are the divisions of Ogham?

Four: B, her five; H, her five; M, her five, and A, her five.

How many sciences in the Ogham are taught, and what are they?

Three: Eight royal or gentle trees; eight kiln trees; and eight spiral trees. The eight royal trees are the Elm, Oak, Hazel, Vine, Ivy, Blackthorn, Broom, Spine; and the eight kiln are the Birch, the Quicken, Willow, Ash, Whitethorn, Fig, Apple and Cork; and the spiral are all from green trees. [N.B. Other lists, from the *Auraicept na nÉces* and Brehon Law, give different ascriptions - see Appendix 3].

How many kinds of Ogham are there?

One hundred and fifty.....First, the branches of the trees are they from whence come the names of the branches in Ogham, [*per alios et alios nominatur*].

By whom and from whence are the veins and beams in the Ogham tree named?

*Per alios*. It came from the school of Phenius through the world, teaching the tongues (he thus employed), in number 25. Noble youths.

From whence come the figures and names in the explanation of B, L and N in Ogham?

From the branches and limbs of the Oak tree: they formed ideas which they expressed in sounds, that is as the stalk of the bush is the noblest part: from them they formed the seven chief figures of the vowels. And they formed three others, which they added to these as helpers, formed on different sides of the line *per alios*, the branches of the wood give figures for the branches and veins in Ogham, chief of all.

The tribe of B, from Birch, and the daughter, that is the ash of the wood, is chief; and from them the first alphabet was formed; of L, namely L, from *Luis*, the Quicken tree of the wood; F, from *Fearn*, alder, good for shields; S from *Sail*, a willow from the wood; N, in Ogham, from *Nin*, the Ash, for spears; H in *Og*. from *Uath*, Whitethorn, a crooked tree, or a bush, because of her thorns; D, from *Dur*, the Oak of fate from the wood; T, from *Tine*, Cypress, or from the Elder Tree; C, in Og. from *Coll*, the Hazel of the wood; Q, in Og. of *Quert*, Apple, Aspen or Mountain Ash; M, from *Mediu* (*Muin*), the Vine, branching finely; G, from *Gort*, namely Ivy towering; Ng, from *Getal*, or *Gilcach*, a reed; St or Z, from *Draighean*, Blackthorn; R, *Graif* [not explained]; A, from *Ailm*, Fir; O, from *On*, the Broom, Furze; U, from *Ur*, Heath; E, from *Edadh*, Aspen trembling; I from *Ida*, or *Ioda*, or *Ioga*, the Yew Tree; EA, *Eabhadh*, the Aspen; OI, *Oir*, the Spine; UI, *Inlleann*, Honeysuckle; IO, the Gooseberry (*Ifin*; AE, the Witch Hazel (*Amhancholl*); Pine Og., that is the divine Pine from the wood, from whence are drawn the four Ifins, or

6. (p.13) *An Ogham Craobh*, the standard 'Tree Ogham' characters, showing *droim* (ridge), *fleasc* (stroke), *fidh* (character), and *aicme* (group).

Vineyards, *per alios*, the name of that branch. The figure resembles the hurdle of wrought twigs, or like a bier".

(Translation by George Mouncey Atkinson, 1872, edited by Nigel Campbell Pennick).

It is clear that a major intention of Ogham's creator was to make a code that could be used to conceal information from those who were not supposed to have it. However, unlike the modern era, when codes exist solely as utilitarian means of keeping information secret, the ancient Celts had no concept of plain utilitarianism. Because they had an ensouled worldview, nothing that they produced was seen as separate, reflecting the complex interactions of things in the world. Thus, with Ogham, whilst remaining very serviceable as a code, it is also a philosophical system in its own right. Although they were chosen arbitrarily, that is, any number or disposition of strokes could have denoted any letter, the originator chose to base the individual characters on trees. The names of the trees already existed, and their initial letters were thus fixed. The qualities and uses of the trees were also fixed. But the order in which the characters were arranged, and their interactive meaning with one another, were created anew when Ogham came into being. With such a code, it is possible to convey vast arrays of meaning through very simple symbols.

## Later Developments

Most contemporary interpretations of Ogham are derived from the seventeenth century Irish bard Roderick O'Flaherty. In his book *Ogygia* (1793), he described the meaning of the Oghams as transmitted to him by Duald MacFirbis, the clan bard of the O'Briens. O'Flaherty's interpretations have been criticized by several prominent Oghamists, especially Dr McAlister. They note that the ascriptions given by O'Flaherty and his followers differed significantly from those in the *Book of Ballymote*, and call them late inventions that have little relationship to the 'original' meanings.

In his *Ogygia*, Roderick O'Flaherty listed the Ogham characters as B, Boibel; L, Loth; F(V), Forann; N, Neiagadon; S, Salia; H, Uiria; D, Daibhaith; T, Teilmon; C, Caoi; CC, Cailep; M, Moiria; G, Gath; Ng, Ngoimar; Y, Idra;; R, Riuben; A, Acab; O, Ose; U, Ura; E, Esu; and I, Jaichim. At least some of the names appear to refer to the Tribes of Israel.

O'Flaherty's system was very influential among esoteric Oghamists of the twentieth century. Two versions of his alphabet were given by Lewis Spence in his book *The Mysteries of Britain* (1928), and, later, they formed the basis for the Ogham theories of Robert Graves. In his highly-influential book, *The White Goddess*, Graves followed O'Flaherty's interpretations, whilst conserving the older names of the Oghams.

In 1977, Colin Murray, leader of the Druidic organization called the Golden Section Order, published literature on the Oghams. It culminated in a divination-card deck published in a limited edition of hand-coloured cards. Along with the cards, Murray published a chart of correspondences that was heavily indebted to Graves's researches (1979). Colin Murray called it "The Divine Game in the Essence" - the sacred play with the planes of human and divine reality". Another work of this period, issued in 1978, was Nigel Pennick's booklet, titled *Ogham and Runic: Magical Writing of Old Britain and Northern Europe*. Also published in that year was Eileen Hogan's *Ogham: Each Letter of the Alphabet is Presented With a Colour and a Bird*. Tree Ogham, Bird Ogham and Colour Ogham, popularized by Robert Graves, remain the three most common forms.

Subsequently, after Murray's tragic early death, his widow Liz published *The Celtic Tree Oracle* (Rider, 1988), which reworked the themes of the earlier Golden Section Order deck. By then, the Oghams had been absorbed fully into contemporary esoteric and Pagan usages.

For the record, it is important to determine as accurately as possible the earliest meanings of the Oghams. But even when they have been determined as well as is humanly possible in the circumstances, this knowledge does not negate necessarily the value of later developments. Devotees of religions often claim that the older a system is, then the closer it is to the 'original', which is thus assumed to be the best and most pure form. This is the essence of all fundamentalisms. However, the nature of existence is change. Everything must evolve from age to age, keeping itself in harmony with the times. Otherwise it will become progressively less useful as time passes, eventually becoming obsolete, and finally passing from being altogether. When we study the past, we must always bear in mind that it is the repository of errors as well as truths, and that, inevitably, new insights have arisen since any system was first organized. They must be accommodated if the system is to remain useful to-day and in the foreseeable future.

7. The island of Ireland can be envisaged as Fionn's Shield, the four provinces corresponding with the four groups of Oghams.

# Chapter 2
# Meanings of the Ogham Feadha

**Types and Order of Ogham**

Ogham is sometimes called the Celtic Tree Alphabet. This is because the basic meanings of the *Feadha* (characters) correspond with certain trees. They are listed in several traditional texts, including the *Book of Ballymote* (1391) and *Ogygia* (1793). Similarly, the Gaelic *Aibítir* has characters that correspond with trees, and the Welsh *Coelbren* is deeply connected with wood-lore. Although there is a generally accepted Ogham correspondence-system, there are variations in recorded historic tree-correspondences for the *Feadha*. The *Auraicept na nÉces* tells of the different interpretations taught by autonomous colleges and independent Bards. Thus, the *Book of Ballymote* lists no fewer than 150 types of Ogham.

The standard, or basic, form of Ogham is *Ogham Craobh*, so-called because the *Feadha* resemble the branches of trees. Its English name is *Branch Ogham*. It is designed to be cut into a hard material, using a *Burin*. Some of the other 149 types are variants of form, with different arrangements of strokes (*Fleasc*). There are Oghams named after things, such as *Righ Ogam*, where each *Fidh* is the name of a king; *Muc Ogam*, where each has a corresponding colour; *En Ogam*, where each is named after one of the ancient bird-names; and *Din Ogam*, 'Hill Ogham', in which each *Fidh* is called after terms connected with a hill. There are also cryptic Oghams, such as

*Ogam Inarbach*, 'The Ogham of Banishment'; *Taeb Ogham Tlachtga*, 'The Side Ogham of Tlachtga'; and *Snaiti Snimach*, 'The Twining, or Tangled Thread'. These, and others are described below. The standard order of Ogham is B, L, F, S, N; H, D, T, C, Q; M, G, Ng, St, R; A, O, U, E, I; Ea, Oi, Ui, Io, Ae. Some texts call the whole row of *An Ogam Craobh*, Beth-Luis-Nion, (B, L, N) which are the first two and the last *Feadha* of the first *Aicme*.

The letter-order given in the *Book of Ballymote* is as in the list above. It begins with the *Feadha* B, L, F. Certain commentators have suggested that the B, L, N order is the older form, and have applied it to their esoteric systems. The idea appears to come from an eighteenth-century antiquary, Dr Ledwich. In his *Antiquities of Ireland* (1792), he states that B, L, N was an early form. But elsewhere Ledwich contradicts himself, writing, "N was anciently the fifth letter". R.A.S. Macalister, in his *The Secret Languages of Ireland* (1937), stated that for some time after its first appearance, the first three letters were B, L, N, and modern esoteric users have taken this B, L, N order for their divinatory systems. They include Colin Murray's original *Ogham Divination Card Game* for the Golden Section Order (1977) and Nigel Jackson's and the present author's *The New Celtic Oracle* (1992 and 1997).

## Ogham Terminology

Ogham has its own terminology, from the Irish. The word Ogham itself means an inscription written or engraved in the characters ascribed to Ogma Grian Ainech. Characters in Ogham are located with relation to a principal stem line or ridge (*Druim* (Scots Gaelic) or *Droim* (Irish Gaeilge: 'back' or 'ridge'). In the earliest Ogham inscriptions on stone, this was actually the corner or edge *Arris* at the junction of two flat surfaces. This *Droim* stem is not a character in its own right, but only a guide. Its upper side is termed the left, and the underside, the right. The individual lines composing the letters are drawn under, over, or through the *Droim*. When the Oghams are cut on a squared stone or stick, then they are cut across the corner angle, which is thus the *Droim*. In Scholastic Ogham, a *Droim* is drawn as a straight line on which the lines are made. The word for these cuts are *Fleasg* (Scots Gaelic) or *Fleasc* (Irish). This means 'rod', 'stave' or 'wand' in Scots Gaelic, with the additional Irish Gaeilge meaning of 'hoop', 'band', 'garland', 'rim' (of a wheel), and also a flask. A line of Ogham characters written along a *Droim* is called *Craobh*, 'a bough', or 'branch'. Each Ogham 'letter', that is, the Ogham equivalent of a letter in an alphabet, is called *Fidh*, 'a tree' (plural, *Feadha*). A Fidh consists of one to five strokes. Each of the *Feadha* is related to a specific tree, and so Ogham is sometimes called the Tree Alphabet. The whole Ogham 'alphabet' together is called *An Ogam Craobh*, 'The Ogham Branch'.

Each of the five groups of Ogham characters is called *Aicme*, 'rubric', 'group', 'class' or 'denomination'. The first three are consonants; the fourth *Aicme* is composed of vowels; whilst the final is of diphthongs. The first *Aicme*, beginning with Beith (BLFSN) is drawn with one to five strokes at right angles below (right of) the *Droim*. The second *Aicme*, that of Huath (HDTCQ), is written with one to five strokes at right angles above (left of) the *Droim*. The third *Aicme*, of Muin (MGNgStR), is made from one to five long strokes cut at an angle across the *Droim*. The fourth *Aicme*, Ailm, (AOUEI), is made of one to five dots or short strokes cutting the *Droim* at right angles. The Feadha of the fifth *Aicme* are known as *Forfeadha* 'Overtrees'. They are late, uncommon, and as a whole *Aicme* of five *Feadha*, may have originated in the time when the *Scholastic Oghams* came into being in monastic *Scriptoria*. They are composed of more complex strokes. Only the first two *Forfeadha* are known from stone inscriptions. Eabhadh (Ea) appears in several Irish inscriptions and in Britain at Crickhowell in Wales. Oir is known from the *Bressay Stone* from Cullingsburgh, Shetland.

8. "Hear the voice of the Bard: Who present, past and future sees. Whose ears have heard, The Holy Word, That walk'd among the ancient trees" William Blake, Songs of Experience, 1794.

Traditionally, since at least the time of the 'Primary Bard of Britain', Taliesin (c. 520 - 570 CE), Celtic Bards of the British Isles have used the kenning 'carpenters of song' for themselves, and other wood-related metaphors for poetry. For example, Taliesin wrote about himself in a poem that refers both to the use of memory and the Ogham script:

> "I am the fund of song,
> I am a reader,
> I love the branches and the tight wattles."

MacLonan, the chief poet of Ireland who died in the year 918 CE, wrote:

> "Cormac of Cashel with his champions,
> Munster is his, may he long enjoy it;
> Around the King of Raith Bicli are cultivated,
> The letters and the trees".

In this poem, the 'letters' (*Litir*) are the characters of the Gaeilge (Irish) Aibítir, whilst the 'trees' (*Feadha*) are the Oghams. Because *An Ogam Craobh*, 'The Ogham Branch' means the whole 'alphabet', by analogy, it can also mean a complete knowledge of all aspects of Ogham, which includes poetry and literature. The Bardic Silver and Golden Branches, carried as emblems of office in ancient Ireland, refer to this high level of learning and creativity. In the *Agallamh an dá Shuadh (The Dialogue of the Two Sages)* we are told that, "Neidhe made his journey with a silver branch over him. The *Anradh*, or poets of the second order, carried a silver branch, but the *Ollamh*, or chief poet, carried a branch of gold; all other poets bore a branch of gold".

In medieval wales, the Bard, Iolo Goch (1315 - 1402 CE), used the wood metaphor to describe his work as coming from the memory and not from written sources:

"I will bear for Owain
In metrical words, fresh and slow,
Continually, not the hewing of Alder (Gwernen) wood,
By the chief carpenter of song".

(For the significance of the Alder, see Fearn below).

In appearance, the Oghams are related to the Scandinavian runic code called *Kvistrunar*, 'twig-' or 'branch-runes'. It appears that this variety of runic encryption came later than the main use of Ogham for memorials, which was between the fourth and eighth centuries CE. It is possible that the Ogham principle was taken up by Scandinavian runemasters living in Ireland, the Isles or Northumbria, and applied by them to the runes. Cryptic runes and possible Oghams exist on a fragment of stone cross kept in the church at Hackness, near Scarborough, Yorkshire. *Kvistrunar* usually encode letters as strokes on either side of an upright stave. The numbers of strokes refer to the number designated to a specific rune in a prearranged sequence.

*Ceart Ogam* ('The Right Ogham') is the Ogham 'alphabet' in the original arrangement ascribed to Ogma; all other versions are said to be variants of this original. In this work, I follow the *Book of Ballymote*. The ascriptions are not all certain. Many of the tree-names are old forms or 'obsolete' Irish. These were interpreted in the nineteenth century by Dr O'Donovan. This uncertainty has also given rise to variations in contemporary interpretation. The variations are described in the appropriate sections below. A description of the meaning of the individual *Feadha* follows.

# An Ogham Craobh

## The First Aicme

### Beith

The first tree of *An Ogam Craobh* is *Beth*, which in modern Irish is *Beith* (Welsh Bedw. This is the Birch Tree, (*Betula pendula*). Its phonetic equivalent is 'B'. The Birch is the the white tree of purification. According to the *Book of Ballymote* and the *Auraicept na nÉces*, wood from a Birch Tree was the substrate upon which the first Ogham word was inscribed. Samuel Taylor Coleridge wrote of the Birch as the 'Lady of the Woods'. The Birch is a pioneer tree, believed to be the first species of tree to recolonize the treeless wastes when the glaciers receded from the British Isles. Birch is a tree of emergence, for, each spring, it is the first deciduous woodland tree to put out leaves. Accordingly, it is classed as the first Peasant or Kiln Tree, with the corresponding colour, Ban (white). In traditional medicine, Birch is an analgesic, used as 'teething twigs' for babies to chew. As an infusion, Birch Tea, it was used in former times to treat kidney stones.

Birch is one of the nine woods used for kindling the ritual *Tein'Eigin* (Need-Fire) and the *Samhnag* (ceremonial bonfire) of *Lá Bealtaine* and *Lá Samhna*. This is noted in a Scottish text in the *Carmina Gaedelica* that tells us to "Choose the Birch of the waterfalls". Birching was used until well into the twentieth century on inmates of British and Manx prisons as corporal punishment. Anciently, it was a means of exorcising evil. Similarly, Birch twigs form part of the traditional besom, used for sweeping away dirt and bad luck (see chapter 5).

Hats made of birch-bark are a sign of the dead. One was found on the remains of the Celtic lord excavated from a sixth century BCE burial mound at Hochdorf near Stuttgart in south Germany. It was a circular, flattened cone. This parallels the words of an English ballad from more than two thousand years later, *The Wife of Usher's Well*. This refers to the birchen hats of the Wife's three dead sons, when they reappear as ghosts. Whether the Birch refers to the Celtic doctrine of transmigration of souls, or is a sign of the purification of the dead, is unknown. The traditional material for babies' cradles is Birch wood.

The Birch is *par excellence* the tree of sexuality. The Bard Dafydd ap Gwilym one of whose lovers, Morfudd ('Goddaughter of May') was a married woman, wrote a poem in which he attempts to convince a nun to come away with him:

> "Is it true, the girl that I love,
> That you do not want Birch, the powerful growth of
>   summer?
> Do not be a nun in springtime,
> Asceticism is not as good as a bush.
> As for the uniform of ring and habit,
> A green dress would ordain better,
> Come to the spreading Birch,
> To the religion of the trees and the cuckoo".

In contemporary Ogham-lore, the Birch-*Fidh* serves to protect against all harm, physical and spiritual. It allows us to deal with bad things; to clear them away, so that a new beginning can take place, unhindered by 'unfinished business'.

**Luis**
The second Ogham *Fidh* is called Luis, whose tree is the Rowan or Quickbeam (*Sorbus acuparia*). Luis is an 'obsolete' feminine Irish name for the tree, which is called *Caorthann* in modern Irish. In Welsh, it is called *Criafol*. The gloss on Luis in the *Book of Ballymote* is *Leam*, meaning 'Elm'.

The Rowan is a tree of hedgerows and woodland, and is the second Peasant or Kiln Tree (but Elm is a Royal or Chieftain

Tree). The *Book of Ballymote* describes the poetic name of Luis as "Delight of the eye, that is Luisiu". This colour is 'flame', the modern Irish *'luisne'*, 'a red glare' (with an inner light, like fire), with the additional meaning of a sheen or lustre. Another colour-correspondence is *Liath*, grey, the mixing of light and darkness.

Rowan is a powerful tree of protection, whose presence at a location suppresses all psychic harm. It is the tutelary tree or 'plant badge' of the Scottish clans MacCallum, MacLachlan, Malcolm and Menzies. In his *Flora Scotica* (1777), John Lightfoot noted that Rowans were plentiful in the vicinity of stone circles in Scotland. Rowans are planted outside the front door of houses to ward off bad luck, baneful magic and autonomous evil. The defensive powers of Rowan are recounted in the traditional Scottish rhyme:

"Rowan tree and red threid
Gar the witches tyne their speed".

Translated into standard English, this is: "Rowan tree and red thread make the witches lose their speed". Magically, Rowan is effective against "the wrath and anger of all men". As a magical protection, Scotswomen traditionally make necklaces out of Rowan berries, strung together on red linen thread.

In the counties on the Anglo-Welsh border, it is customary to make crosses of Birch and Rowan twigs, tied with red thread. They are placed over doors on May morning, and left in place until the next May Day. In Scotland, Rowan rods are used in the same way. In horse-drawn days, Rowan was used for the horsemen's switches or whips used to subdue 'bewitched' horses. Rods of Rowan were used in rhabdomancy for finding metals hidden beneath the earth. Festal cakes or bannocks baked over a fire of Rowan wood are considered to have apotropaic powers.

9. Crannogs, lake villages and cities like Rotterdam were built on the Ogham Fearn, resistant piles of the Alder Tree.

Mythologically, Rowan brings magical transformation. The Irish tale of *The Wooing of Etain* tells how Queen Fuamnach, wife of the underworldly Midir, hits Etain with a Rowan rod. Immediately, Etain is transformed into a pool of water, then a worm and a fly which generates a heavenly fragrance and sweet music.

In contemporary usage, Luis serves to protect its user against psychic attack. It is used for the development of the power of second sight, and self-control against inner anger. In a divination, Luis warns that the subject is under external psychic stress, with the proviso that if he or she takes the appropriate precautions, then there will be no harm.

## Fearn

The third Ogham *Fidh* is Fearn, 'F'. Fearn corresponds with the Alder Tree, (*Alnus glutinosa*). Fearn is masculine in Irish Gaeilge, but feminine in Scottish Gaelic. In modern Irish, Alder is called *Fearnóg* (the Welsh *Gwernen*). Fearn also means 'a shield' and 'the mast of a ship'. It is related to the word *Fearsad,* which can mean 'a shaft', 'an axle', 'the ulna bone' or 'a narrow sea passage'. As 'shaft', it refers to the Alder piles which were used all over Europe for the foundations of buildings in wetlands. Alder wood is the best timber for this purpose. The foundations of wetland cities such as Venice and Rotterdam, lowland cathedrals like Winchester, watermills, lake villages and the island *crannogs* of the British Isles were built upon piles of Alder. Symbolically, Fearn is a tree of fire used to free the earth from water. On a human scale, protection against the wet ground comes in the shape of Alder-wood clogs for the feet. It also provides the wood used in making the 'magic whistles' used to 'whistle up the wind'.

In traditional crafts, Alder wood was used for making milk pails and other containers used in the dairy. The *Word Ogham* of Mac ind Og gives Fearn's kenning as "guarding of milk".

Although Fearn has the interpretation 'shield', from the *Book of Ballymote*, "good for shields", it seems that in the days before firearms, Alder was used as a second-best alternative to wood from the Linden Tree. According to ancient chronicles and sagas, both the Anglo-Saxon and Scandinavian warriors favoured shields made from Limewood, covered with leather.

In the smithy, this tree of fire was an essential part of sword-making. Swordsmiths prized Alder wood because it furnished the best charcoal for metal-smelting. In later times, its military connection was continued with the new technology of gunpowder-production, for Alder charcoal was the best ingredient. *The Song of the Forest Trees* describes Alder as "The very battle-witch of all woods, the tree that is hottest in the fight". In contemporary usages, Fearn is best used for personal protection in conflicts, and for freeing oneself from magical bindings of every kind.

The *Fidh* Fearn is associated with the colour called *Flann*, blood-red or crimson. This is because when an Alder tree is cut down, its sap turns red like blood. Like the Yew, the Alder is seen as a 'bleeding tree', and so, in traditional belief, to fell an Alder tree is a sacrilege which will bring retribution in the form of the transgressor being burnt out of house and home. In traditional crafts, the Alder provides fabric dyes. Three dyes can be prepared from the Alder Tree. The bark makes red; the twigs make brown; and the flowers make green. These Fearn dyes were the basic colours for the ancient plaid patterns which evolved into the Scottish tartans of the present day.

In British mythology, the Alder Tree is connected with King Bran, whose mummified oracular head was carried around Britain. Finally, his followers buried it at Bryn Gwyn, the White Mount of Trinovantium, now occupied by the Norman White Tower of the Tower of London. There, until it was dug up by King Arthur, it served as the magical shield of Britain against her enemies. According to Robert Graves in *The White Goddess*, the 'singing head' of Bran symbolizes the 'head' of the Alder tree, the topmost branch. This 'head' is visible in winter, when the tree had lost its leaves. Then the Alder's black cones and unopened catkins give the tree a dense, purple-tinged crown.

## Saille

Saille, phonetically, 'S', corresponds with the Sally Tree (White Willow *Salix alba*). In the old Irish Brehon Law, the name for this tree is given as *Sail*, and in modern Irish, *Saileach* (in Welsh, it is *Helygen*). The Sally Tree is the third of the Peasant or Kiln Trees. Its corresponding colour in *Muc Ogham* is *Sodath*, interpreted as 'bright' or 'fine'. The Sally Tree loves water and grows close to pools, streams and rivers.

In traditional medicine, the bark of the Sally Tree provided relief from the disorders and diseases of dampness, such as headache, the ague, rheumatism and arthritis. Its young osiers are pliant, finding many uses in basket-, wattle- and hurdle-making. It is used as a binding-material in thatched roofs; in wattle-and-daub walling, and also as the withies used to bind the Birch twigs onto the broomstick of traditional Besoms. When the Welsh 'wood-alphabet' called *Coelbren Y Beirdd* was revived during King Henry IV's persecution of Welsh culture after 1400, it was the basket-makers who were the keepers of the tradition.

As well as being pliant when young, when mature, Willow is a resonant wood. In traditional craft, the Willow provides the material for the sound-box of the *Cláirseach* (Irish Harp), and the blades of English cricket bats. It is one of the nine woods used in the *Tein'Eigin* and the bonfires of May and November, though *The Song of the Forest Trees* tells us, "Burn not the willow, a tree sacred to poets".

In contemporary Ogham lore, Saille is a *Fidh* of being pliant, the flowing, watery symbolism of coming into harmony naturally with the flow of events, most notably the phases of the Moon. In divination, its power is greater in darkness than in daylight, except when the Moon is visible during the day. Its power fluctuates with the cycle of the Moon's phases.

**Nin**

Nin, Nuin or Nion is the last letter of the first *Aicme*. It has the phonetic value of 'N', and corresponds with the Ash Tree (*Fraxinus excelsior*). "Nin, the Ash, for spears", as the *Book of Ballymote* tells us. The *Book of Ballymote* also has the gloss, *Nendait*, which may mean 'Nettle', for Nin, and the gloss *Uinseann* (Ash) for the *Fidh* Ur.

The Ash is the fourth Peasant or Kiln Tree. In the Brehon Laws, it is *Iundius*, and its modern Irish name is *Fuinnseog*, and in Welsh *Onnen*. The colour associated with Nion is *Necht*, 'clear'. Ash is valued because it is fast-growing, giving a hard-wearing wood better than any other European tree. The wood is heavy, strong, but with a certain elasticity. It takes a fine polish, and bends well when seasoned. An Ash beam will take a heavier load, *pro rata* than any other tree. In former times, Ash was the wood of choice for makers of military spear-shafts, and it is still used for making the now-illegal otter-spears. Magically, Ash is used in charming away warts.

Of Ash, *The Song of the Forest Trees* tells us:

> Ash logs, smooth and grey,
> Burn them green or old,
> Buy up all that come your way -
> Worth their weight in gold."

According to contemporary insights, the Ash is the tree of rebirth, linking that which is above with that which is below, the worlds of the spirit and of matter. It is the passage between the inner world and the outer world. Symbolically, the bunches of fruits that resemble and are called 'Keys' signify the power to unlock future events. But, just as the seeds in these keys germinate only in the second year after falling to the ground, unlocking the future may not be instant.

## The Second Aicme

### Huath

The first *Fidh* of the second *Aicme* is Huath, sometimes rendered as hUath or Uath, with the phonetic value of 'H'. 'H' is absent from Irish Gaeilge and Scots Gaelic. It is used only as an aspirant before an initial vowel, or in foreign 'loan-words' for which there is no equivalent. Another meaning of *Uath* is as a numeral substantive, meaning 'a unit', anything single. In Ogham lore, Huath signifies the Whitethorn or Hawthorn Tree, (*Crataegus monogyna*), "a crooked tree, or a bush, because of her thorns". Brehon Law calls this three Sceith. In modern Irish, this tree is called *Sceach gheal*, and in Welsh, *Ysbyddaden* or *Draenenwen*. A gloss in the *Book of Ballymote* gives Rge as an alternative name for this character.

The Hawthorn is the fifth Peasant or Kiln Tree whose colour, hUath, 'terrible', is interpreted in modern terms as purple. Another name for this thorn tree is the May Tree, and Huath's blossoms in the Merry Month of May. The blooming of the May Tree was the marker of *Lá Bealtaine* (Beltane, May Day), rather than a calendar date. This is remembered in the old English adage, "Ne'er cast a clout, till May be out" (do not cast off your winter clothes until you see a May Tree blossom). Traditionally, it is unlucky to bring May blossom into the house.

Traditional craftsmen prized wood from the roots of Hawthorn for making combs and boxes, for the wood is fine-grained and

10. Celtic holy wells are enhanced by the power of the Thorn and other holy trees that grow alongside them.

takes a brilliant polish. Hawthorn wood burns with the hottest flame, and Hawthorn charcoal is reputed to give out more heat than that of other woods. An ancient meaning of *hUath* is 'dreadful', 'terrible', or 'horrible', referring to its daunting thorny nature. The *Auraicept na néces* tells us, "A meet of hounds is *huath*....because it is formidable, owing to its thorns". This meaning of 'thorn' is identical with the meaning of the Germanic, Anglo-Saxon and Norse Rune called variously *Thurisaz* or *Thorn*, which has a daunting, defensive, quality.

In 1485, it was from a thorn bush at Bosworth Field that the crown from the helmet of the slain King Richard III was brought to the Welsh lord, Henry Tudor, who thus proclaimed himself king Henry VII of England and Wales. Subsequently, Henry VII's 'plant badge' was the Hawthorn. In contemporary understanding, Huath is the Ogham *Fidh* of protection against all ills, invoking the power of the Otherworld.

In Irish folk tradition, this tree is considered to be a 'Gentle' or 'Fairy' tree (not to be confused with the epithet 'Gentle' as meaning Royal or Chieftain). It brings extreme misfortune to anyone foolhardy enough to tamper with one. The death of one's children or livestock and the loss of all of one's money is the traditional fate of such an individual. The lore of Thorn Trees is dealt with at length in Chapter 5.

## Duir

The *Fidh*, Duir, corresponds with the Common or Pedunculate Oak (*Quercus robur* - in modern Irish *Dair* and in Welsh, *Derwen*). It has the phonetic value of 'D'. Duir is the second Royal or Chieftain Tree (after Elm, the 'gloss' of Luis). Its colour is *Dubh*, black. Throughout Europe, the Oak is considered to be the most powerful tree of all, "the Oak of fate from the wood". It is invariably the holy tree of the sky-god, called in different places, Zeus, Dispater, Jupiter, Taranis, Daronwy, the Dagda, Perun, Perkunas, Ziu, Thunor and Thor.

11. The Wren Boys make their annual ceremonial outing on St Stephen's Day (Boxing Day, December 26), having travelled many miles, over hedges and stiles in search of their 'king' (inset).

The Oak was the holy tree of the Celtic Druids, and its name, Duir is related to the Irish words *Dúr*, 'hard', 'unyielding', 'durable'; and *Dúrunta*, 'mysterious'. It is cognate with other words for 'door' in various European languages: the Irish Doras, Greek Thura, and the German Tür, etc. As *Cád Goddeu* (The Battle of the Trees) tells us: "Stout door-keeper against the foe is his name in all lands". The gloss on *Dair* from Brehon Law is "size, beauty, acorns for pigs".

The Oak is the 'plant badge' of the Irish O'Connors and several Scottish clans, including Clan Buchannan, Cameron and Cameron of Lochiel, Kennedy and Stewart. It is the 'crest badge' of the Andersons (MacAndrews) and Clan MacEwen (the House of Bardrochat), which shows a cut-off Oak trunk from which new sprouts are growing. The Cornish surname Derrick is from *Derowek*, an Oak grove.

The bird of this *Fidh* is relevant to the king of all trees, for it is *Droen*, the Wren, called "the king of all birds" though one of the smallest of all indigenous birds in Europe. It was a sacred bird of the Druids, and there was an ancient *Geis* against killing Wrens. The *Geis* continued in post-Pagan times, except on St Stephen's Day (Boxing Day, December 26), when the Wren Boys hunted and killed a Wren, and then paraded it around, singing the local *Wren Boys' Song*. The custom exists throughout the British Isles and Brittany, and, although Wrens are no longer killed, the tradition is maintained, from the performance of *The Cutty Wren* in England to the *Bodhrán*-playing Wrenboys of Ireland. The Wren Boys' Song from the Englishry of Pembrokeshire begins with the invocation, "Joy, health, love and peace, be all here in this place", and goes on to tell of the difficulties involved in catching the Wren, "We have travelled many miles, over hedges and stiles, in search of our king". In Welsh-speaking Denbighshire and Flintshire, *Can Hela'r Dryw* is sung, and, on the Isle of Man, *Shelg Y Drean*. The Irish version, sung in English, tells us:

"The Wren, the Wren, the king of all birds,
On Stephen's day was caught in the Furze.
Though he was little his honour was great
So give us a penny to give us a treat.....
Up with the kettle and down with the pan,
And give us a penny to bury the Wren."

The Wren is the 'bird badge' of the Pennick family.

To the contemporary understanding, this important *Fidh* signifies strength. Things of great strength are sometimes hidden from view, like the 'Bog Oaks' buried beneath the peat in the bogs of Ireland and the Fens of East Anglia. But, once found, they can be recovered and be of great service. Spiritually, Duir may serve as a psychic doorway to inner experiences. Duir enables us to see the invisible, and also to become unseen; to allow entry of those who should enter and to exclude those who ought not. Further Oak lore can be found in chapters 4 and 5.

**Tinne**
With a phonetic value of 'T', Tinne, Tine or Tindi is given by the *Book of Ballymote* as corresponding with the Cypress Tree (*Cupressus sp.*), Rowan (*Sorbus acuparia*). In addition, a *Book of Ballymote* gloss gives it as *Trom* (Elder, *Sambucus nigra*). Modern Oghamists usually associate it with the Holly (*Ilex aquifolium*). However a gloss in the *Book of Ballymote* associates Holly (*Quilleann*) with the *Fidh* Quert (see below).

Because of this multiple ascription, there is some confusion as to the meaning of Tinne. The Rowan tree is more commonly identified with Luis, (*Caorthann*). However, the modern Irish word for Holly is *Cuileann*, cognate with the Welsh name, *Celyn*. Its Scots Gaelic counterpart has the literal meaning of the name, 'fire', which is related to Holly (and Rowan) by its fire-red berries, as in the *Word Ogham* kenning of Mac ind Og, *Smair guaili*, 'fires of coal'. Holly wood does burn exceptionally well. In *Cád Goddeu* (*The Song of the Forest Trees*) we are reminded, "Holly logs will burn like wax, you may burn them green".

As fire and as Holly, the *Fidh* has the meaning of 'warmth', 'shelter' and 'protection' (against the elements). In a twelfth-century *Suibhne* poem, the Wild-Man-like eponymous hermit gives Holly the kenning, "little shelterer, door against the wind". Holly sticks are used in the Irish children's Hallowe'en game called 'Building the House', where twelve pairs of sticks are arranged in a circle, thrust into the ground, brought together at the top, and tied. The coupled twigs are named after the boys and girls present at the game. Then a burning turf is placed at the centre of the circle, and the first pair of twigs that catch fire denotes which boy and girl will be the first to marry."

Holly is the tree most associated with the traditional British Yuletide festivities, being called Christ's Thorn in some northern dialects. It crowns Old Father Christmas, and appears in the ancient carol, *The Holly and the Ivy*, where its berries are "as red as any blood". In certain parts of Wales, Holly, which as *Cád Goddeu* recalls, is "defended with spikes on every side", was used to draw blood in a Yuletide custom whose meaning is uncertain. The custom of *Holly Beating* or *Holming Day* was observed on St Stephen's Day (Boxing Day, December 26). In the nineteenth century, it was described in Tenby, Pembrokeshire, as "a furious onslaught, made by boys and men, armed with large bushes of prickly Holly, on the naked and unprotected arms of female domestics and others of a like class" (*Tales and Traditions of Tenby*, 1858). This aspect of midwinter misrule was suppressed by the Tenby police in 1857, and by similar actions elsewhere. Perhaps related to *Holly Beating* is its part in the martial arts, where it is portrayed as the club of the Wild Man.

Holly is the 'plant badge' of several Scottish clans: Drummond, MacInnes, Mackenzie and Macmillan. The 'crest badge' of the Maxwells shows a stag standing in front of a Holly bush.

Traditional crafts use the hard white wood of the Holly in several ways. The *Auraicept na nÉces* tells how it was "one of the three timbers of the chariot wheel". Holly is good for the stocks of light driving-whips and walking-sticks, as well as the cudgels and clubs employed by practitioners of the northern European martial arts. Crooked branches of Holly were used as 'crook-sticks' for suspending the cauldron over the fire. A strong wood, Holly can withstand both the heat of the fire and the load of the cauldron and its contents, without breaking. In former times, small clinker-built Irish fishing boats had keels made of Holly wood because it wears smooth and slides well on gravel beaches. In pre-industrial days, Holly printing-blocks were used to print fabrics.

In contemporary usage, Tinne is a *Fidh* of unification, employed for personal might and main, used in a balanced manner. It has a strong male element, which is connected specifically with fatherhood and posterity.

**Coll**
The fourth Ogham *Fidh* of the second *Aicme* is Coll, with the phonetic value of 'K' or a hard 'C'. It signifies the "Hazel of the wood", (*Corylus avellana*), the third Royal or Chieftain Tree. Its ancient name is the same in modern Irish, whilst in Welsh it is Collen. The *Auraicept na nÉces* tells us that in the *Word Ogham* of Morann mac Main, Hazel is "*Cainiu fedalb,* the fairest of trees", and in *Mac ind Og's Ogham*, it is *Cara bloisc*, 'the friend of cracking' (presumably from its fruit, known sometimes as *Filbert Nuts*). Brehon Law glosses Coll "for nuts and rods" and also numbers it among the Chieftain Trees. According to country lore, the Hazel first produces nuts only after nine years' growth.

Hazel is a tree of knowledge. According to Irish myth, over Connla's Well, in County Tipperary, grew the nine Hazels of Wisdom and Inspiration, the Hazels of the science of poetry, "out of which were obtained the feats of the sages". The Heralds of ancient Ireland carried white Hazel wands as symbols of office, representing their ability to use words and giving them free passage as non-combatants. At royal inaugurations in Ireland, the Fili gave the king a a wand of Hazel as a sign of his accession.

More recently, in Wales, the white Hazel was involved in the hurtful custom of sending the *Ffon Wen* ('White Stick') anonymously to a rejected lover. This revelation of the truth would take place on or near the wedding-day of his or her former partner. The *Ffon Wen* was a freshly-peeled Hazel stick, sometimes trimmed with a black ribbon bow, and accompanied by insulting rhymes. In later years, they were sent by the Royal Mail. The custom continued longest in western Montgomeryshire.

According to *Silva Gadelica* and E. Hull's *Folklore of the British Isles* (1928), many British and Irish sacred places were originally Hazel groves. In the early medieval period, Hazel poles were used to delimit the ritual enclosure known by the Old Norse name of *Hoslur* or the English *Enhazelled Field*. In Norse terminology, these round-headed poles were called *Tjosnar*. Once a field had been enhazelled, then the formal rules of battle applied there. Both in the single combat called *Holmganga* and in full-scale formal battles between armies, the 'theatre of conflict' was cut off from the normal world of everyday life by Hazel posts which formed a boundary around it. The modern boxing ring and all rectangular sports fields such as those used for Association, Rugby and American football are descendants of the Enhazelled Field by way of the *Lists* of the medieval tournament.

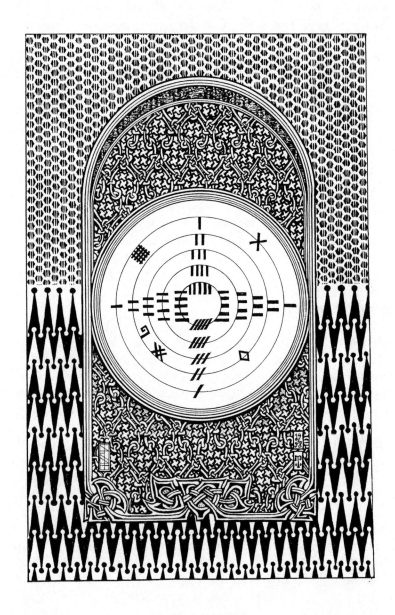

12. *Fionn's Shield*

Hazel is a tree whose wood can be used magically. The medieval *Book of St Albans* records a magical technique for invisibility that employs a Hazel rod one and a half Fathoms in length (nine English feet; 2.7432 metres). A green Hazel twig is implanted in its end. Another magic Hazel implement is recalled in the Irish legend of *The Ancient Dripping Hazel*. In this story, a certain magic Hazel Tree dripped venom. Fionn MacCumhaill cut down the tree and made it into a shield that emitted poisonous gases that killed his enemies. *Fionn's Shield* is a poetic kenning for magical protection by a diagram containing all of the *Feadha* of Ogham. It also means a satirical poem which carries a curse on the subject of the satire.

In his *The Description of Wales* (1193), Geraldus Cambrensis write how Welsh people kept their teeth spotlessly clean with Hazel twigs, and forked Hazel twigs were used by rhabdomants in water divining. Here, the Hazel was another means of 'finding out'. In ancient Ireland, the intoxicating drink, Hazel Mead, was prized for its qualities. In Scotland, the 'plant badge' of the Colquhouns is the Hazel, and the Cornish surnames Collett and Collick refer to Hazel trees.

The contemporary interpretation of Coll is as a *Fidh* of clear perception and inspired consciousness

## Quert

The final *Fidh* of the second *Aicme* is contentious. Standing for 'Q' is Quert, generally taken to mean the Crab Apple tree (*Malus sylvestris*). It is the seventh Kiln or Peasant Tree of the *Ogham Craobh*. However, the *Book of Ballymote* also gives two alternative ascriptions for Quert: Aspen and Rowan, whilst a gloss in another section ascribes Q as Quilleann, Holly. The 'obsolete' Irish, Quert, appears to be a version of the Scots Gaelic *Cuirt*, which means 'Apple'. Modern Irish calls the Apple *Aball*, and Welsh, *Afal*. Quert's colour is given variously as Apple-green and *Quiar*, mouse-coloured.

Legends from various parts of Europe show that the Apple is symbolic of eternal life. The Greek tradition tells of the Golden Apples of the Hesperides, the Norse speaks of the goddess Iduna and the apples of immortality, whilst Celtic tradition has the Isle of Avalon, to which King Arthur is taken after his last battle, to heal his wounds. Perhaps to symbolize the after-life, at the funeral of Velters Cornewall of Moccas in Herefordshire, April 1768, twelve women walked in the funeral cortège carrying Apple-tree branches.

Symbolically, the five strokes to the left of the stem of the Ogham *Fidh* can be seen as reflecting the fivefold petals of the Apple flower, and the five receptacles for the seeds within the fruit itself. Unlike the cultivated species of Apple, the Crab Apple is a thorn-bearing tree, giving Quert protective qualities. The Crab-Apple is the 'plant badge' of the Scots Clan Lamont.

## The Third Aicme

### Muin
Muin or Min has a phonetic value of 'M', and is usually ascribed to the Grape vine, the 'obsolete' Irish *Mediu*, "the Vine branching finely" (*Vitis*) However, in modern Irish, the Grapevine is Finúim. This plant is not indigenous to the British Isles, but it was grown in climatically favourable parts of Britain during the Roman occupation, and wine plays an integral part in Christian ritual.

Muin is the fourth Royal or Chieftain Tree. However, in the Irish language, *Muine* has the meaning of 'a thicket' of any thorny plant, so the correlation of this Ogham with the grape vine may not be so strong. Its corresponding colour is *Mbracht*, 'variegated'.

According to contemporary interpretation, Muin denotes the ability to range over a wide area and gather together everything we need. Once gathered together, they are assimilated into us, aiding our inner development.

## Gort

The *Fidh* Gort has the phonetic value of 'G'. It represents the Ivy (*Hedera helix*), "Ivy towering" in the *Book of Ballymote*, the fifth Royal Tree. Ivy is *Eadhnéan* in modern Irish. In Welsh, the name of this 'tree' is *Eiddew*. But the meaning of this *Fidh* is problematical, for the Irish word *Gort* means a tilled field, not Ivy. Also, a gloss in the *Book of Ballymote* gives the word *Gius*, meaning 'Mistletoe'. What the two plants have in common is that they both grow on other trees. The Ivy roots in the ground, but twines round tall trees for support, whilst the Mistletoe roots between the branches of trees and grows as a semi-parasite. *Gorm* (blue), is the colour associated with Gort. Ivy is the 'plant badge' of the Gordon clan.

According to contemporary interpretation, Gort represents the changes that are necessary for growth, and the requirement that all things be related to the Earth. Just as it is necessary to till the fields in order to reap a harvest later, so it is necessary to do the 'groundwork' in anything before we can reap the benefits. Although the Ivy uses other plants or walls for support, to survive, it must remain rooted in the ground. Beginning as a small, weak, herb-like plant, it grows slowly over many years to become an enormously thick, woody, serpentine tree in its own right. Because the name of this *Fidh* is related to the Irish *Gorta*, meaning 'hunger' or 'famine', it may give an unfavourable reading in an Ogham divination. Unfavourably, Gort can indicate scarcity, the failure of the tilled field to produce an adequate harvest.

## Ngetal

The thirteenth *Fidh* is Ngetal or Ngedal, 'Ng', *Getal*, the Reed. In Irish its modern name is *Giolcach*, and in Welsh *Cawnen*.

13. According to Bardo-Druidic teachings, Nwvvre, symbolized by the Wyvern, a two-legged dragon, is the underlying subtle quality that empowers existence.

The Reed is the first of the Kiln or Shrub trees. Its colour is Nglas, usually thought of as 'glass green', a clear yellowish-green. A *Book of Ballymote* gloss gives *Gilcach*, 'Broom', for this *Fidh*.

It may appear strange that the Irish Bards called the Reed a tree, but the contemporary definition of what is and what is not a tree is a relatively recent scientific convention. In traditional perception and language, different criteria prevail. The most obvious example is the many kinds of fish described by the English language which are not classified as fish (*Pisces*) at all by scientific taxonomists: shell-fish, jelly-fish, cray-fish and whale-fish. According to traditional definitions, any plant with woody stems, such as a Reed or Ivy, is a tree. It seems that in ancient times, the Irish scribes classified the Reed as a tree because its hard, resistant stems make good pens. The Welsh scribes' favourite material, *Plagawd*, was also made from reeds.

Ngetal is a preserver: as a pen, the Reed preserves memory and knowledge, as a rod, it preserves measure, and as roofing it preserves the house. The traditional use of the Reed is as a covering, for weatherproofing the roof of the house with Reed thatch, and, as a floor-covering, especially in winter, when Reeds served as insulation. As a Bardic tree, however, Ngetal is the *Fidh* of written communication, thereby maintaining human culture over time.

The many uses of the reed in traditional society are reflected in its contemporary symbolic meanings. In addition to signifying preservation, Ngetal denotes the flexibility that we must possess if we are to survive in the prevailing circumstances without sacrificing our integrity. From its use in thatching, and as the covert in which birds take refuge, it is the container and protector of living things, just as writing is the container and protector of thought and culture.

## Straif

The fourteenth *Fidh* is called Straif or Straiph. With the phonetic equivalent 'St' (or 'Z'), it signifies the Blackthorn or Sloe tree, *Prunus spinosa*, which is counted as the sixth Royal Tree. Its old Irish name was *Droigion* (*Draidean* in Brehon Law, modernly, *Draíon* or *Draighnean*), and in Welsh, it is *Draenenwen*. Straif's corresponding colour is *Sorcha*, 'bright coloured'. Blackthorn is a tree of power, whose name has the connotations of 'punishment' and 'strife'. Staves made from its wood, carried by witches, warlocks and wizards, have always been renowned for their magical power. The Irish word for a 'Wizard', *Draoi*, and that of a Druid, *Draí*, are both indicative of the 'turning' power of the Blackthorn.

Physically, the Sloe Tree has a very hard and durable wood, excellent for making walking-sticks, shillelaghs, cudgels and the 'Black Rod' of wizards. It is a fine plant for making hedges, with formidable thorns that make an impenetrable barrier. Blackthorn produces suckers which, as the years pass, grow to make a single plant the nucleus of an impenetrable thorny thicket. Medicinally, the fruit of the Blackthorn is the key component in Sloe Gin.

The contemporary view of Straif in magic and divination sees it as a provider of power on both the material and non-material levels. Straif gives strength and determination to the willpower: it contains the strength we need to resist and defeat adversity, and to control or ward off magical attack. Thus it is considered the most powerful *Fidh* for overthrowing all resistance to one's will.

## Ruis

Ruis, with the phonetic value of 'R' corresponds with the Elder Tree or Bourtree (*Sambucus nigra*). In the Brehon Law and in modern Irish, this is *Trom* and in Welsh *Ysgaw*). The name 'Ruis' is cognate with the Irish word Rúisc, which means a violent attack, a blow, or a throw. This expresses the protective but dangerous nature of this holy tree. The bark and flowers of the Elder possess healing properties, but the vapours that accumulate in Elder woodland are reputed to produce disease and even bring death to those who might linger there for too long. Perhaps it is significant that Walter Tyrell, the archer who killed the Norman King, William II Rufus, shot him from beneath an Elder tree. The colour ascribed to Ruis is *Rocnat*, one of the many forms of red recognized in pre-scientific days. The Cornish surnames Scawn and Scown refer to the Elder Tree, *Scawen* in the Cornish tongue.

In certain parts of the British Isles, it is considered extremely inauspicious to burn Elder wood in a house. Flowering branches of Elder, however, are effective in warding off flies from byres and stables. As a tree of magic in Ireland, Elder sticks were reputed to have been the steeds of witches in place of the more common besoms or hurdles. The Elder is the origin of two medicinal alcoholic beverages which ward off the cold and illness: Elder-flower wine, brewed in June and July from the creamy-white flowers, and Elder-berry wine, fermented from the purple-black fruits that ripen in August and September.

According to contemporary sensibilities, Ruis signifies the three aspects of time present in the Three Fates. As the Weird Sisters, they represent the ever-present threefold aspects of existence: beginning, middle and end. Ruis denotes the acceptance all three aspects that we must have if we are to lead balanced lives. Ruis is thus a *Fidh* of timelessness, expressed as the unity of all time.

# The Fourth Aicme

**Ailm**

Ailm, the Elm Tree (*Ulmus minor*), is the first *Fidh* of the fourth *Aicme*. It is the first Royal or Chieftain Tree in the *Book of Ballymote*. Ailm has the phonetic value of 'A'. The kind of Elm represented by this Ogham *Fidh* is the western variety known commonly as the 'Cornish Elm' (*Ulmus minor, var stricta*). Before the 1970s, when Elms in the British Isles were devastated by Dutch Elm Disease, this variety was common in Cornwall, Devon and South-Western Ireland. Unlike most Elms, this is a wayside tree that does not grow in woodland. This *Fidh* is probably cognate with the Scots Gaelic alphabet *Litir*, *Fhailm*, meaning 'Elm'. Brehon Law calls Elm, *Leam*.

The ascription of Ailm to Elm is not always used by Oghamists, however, because in the 'obsolete' Irish of the *Book of Ballymote* the correspondence has been interpreted as 'Fir' (with a gloss of *Aball*, Apple). Brehon Law reckons Fir as one of the seven Chieftain Trees, calling it Ochtach, "wood for supporting posts". The twentieth-century Bards Robert Graves and Colin Murray associated this *Fidh* with the European Silver Fir (*Abies alba*), the tallest species of Fir Tree. But there are objections to this as well: 'Fir' in this context may well refer to what is, in botanical terms, Pine. There is certainly a link in Welsh tradition, for in *Cád Goddeu* we are told of the "Pine Trees in the court" that "the Elm Trees are his subjects...".

However, this species of Fir is not indigenous to the British Isles. The Irish word for a Fir tree is *Giúis*. The meaning if confused further by the possibility that the ancient Ailm could be a version of the modern *Pailm*, 'a Palm Tree'. Although Palms are not indigenous to northern Europe, they have a connection with Christian iconography, and will grow in the milder parts of the British Isles. Palm Trees are notable features of some ancient churchyards in south Wales, including Penally and Llantwit Major. How long Palms have been cultivated in the British Isles is not known. Its corresponding colour is usually given as blue.

In the contemporary view, Ailm represents the towering strength that we need to rise above adversity. Like the tallest tree, we can have the viewpoint of a higher level, bringing us a better perception of future trends. If we take the Elm parallel, then it is a *Fidh* of regeneration. The Elm can regrow from new shoots that arise from the roots. When an Elm is cut down, and seemingly dead, new stems grow from the still-living roots. This has happened in the case of trees suffering from Dutch Elm Disease.

## On

On or Onn is the second Ogham vowel, with the phonetic value of 'O', corresponding with the Gorse, Broom, or Furze (*Ulex europaeus*). This is the seventh Royal or Chieftain Tree of *An Ogham Craobh*. The modern Irish word for the Gorse is *Aiteann* (Brehon Law, *Aidteand*) cognate with the Welsh *Eithin*. The Old Irish gloss on Onn is *Ferus*, 'Furze'. The Gorse grows only in open country, not in woodland. It flowers in almost every month of the year, so it is a symbol of unending fertility. The colour of On is that of the Gorse flowers, described variously as golden-yellow, saffron, dun or sand. Gorse is the 'plant badge' of the Scottish Logan clan.

According to contemporary interpretations, On signifies the carrying-on of our activities in spite of adverse surrounding conditions. This is a way of life that involves 'standing out' against the background in the same way that the Gorse shows up in the landscape. Symbolically, On denotes the collecting together and retention of our inner strength, regardless of the outer conditions. Because the seeds of Gorse are dispersed by ants, this *Fidh* expresses the necessity for gathering small and separate things together.

**Ur**
Ur, Ura or Up is the third vowel, corresponding with the Heather (*Erica sp.*), in the *Book of Ballymote, Ur*. Ur is another problematical *Fidh*, as Brehon Law calls this plant *Freach* (modern Irish, *Fraoch*; Welsh *Grug*. A *Book of Ballymote* gloss also gives the correspondence *Uinseann*, 'Ash'. Ur has the literal meaning of 'fresh', 'new', or 'moist', with the associated meaning of the morning dew. Heather is considered to be an extremely lucky plant. To this day it is sold in the streets by itinerant sellers as a luck-bringer. Its traditional corresponding colour is purple, the colour of its flowers.

Contemporary interpretation sees Ur bringing good forune and and freshness to any venture to which it is applied. Ur serves as a portal to inner worlds. In his Druidic teachings in the Golden Section Order, Colin Murray linked this Ogham *Fidh* with Mistletoe (*Viscum album*), as well as the Heather. He saw the Mistletoe as a complementary aspect of the *Fidh*, signifying the power of regeneration and healing.

**Edadh**
Edadh or Eadha is the fourth vowel, phonetically 'E', corresponding with the Aspen or White Poplar Tree (*Populus tremula*). A gloss in the *Book of Ballymote* also gives *Eden*, 'Ivy', for this *Fidh*. In Scottish Gaelic, the corresponding *Litir* of the alphabet is called Eubh, whose tree is also the Aspen. The modern Irish name for the Aspen is *Pobail ban*, and in Welsh, it is *Aethnen*. The Aspen is a very hardy tree. It thrives in a diverse range of habitats, from low-lying wetlands to exposed mountain ledges. In former times, its trembling white leaves made people plant it as a very visible way- or boundary-marker.

The esoteric view of Edadh is that it expresses the quality of hardihood and fierce resistance to a variety of seemingly-inhospitable conditions. Thus, it is seen as a preventer of death. It facilitates our curative powers, providing direct access to the real essence that underlies the sometimes misleading outer form. Edadh is the spirit than animates the flesh. At its most powerful, it signifies our willpower overriding our fate. It contains the possibility that the power of the mind can overcome the inertia of matter, warding off death.

**Ida**

The *Fidh* variously called Ida, Idha, Idad, Idho, Ioda, Ioho, Ioga or Iubhar is the Yew tree (*Taxus baccata*), with the phonetic value 'I'. In the Brehon Laws, it is called *Ibor*, and in modern Irish, it is *Eo*, the Welsh, *Yw*. In the Scottish Gaelic *Aibítir*, it is Iubhar, the second Yew of that alphabet. The Ogham *Fidh* is connected directly with the rune called Eihwaz in the 24-rune Elder Futhark, which has the form of a double-ended stave of death and life. In medieval Europe, longbows, staves of death, were made of Yew. An old Irish kenning for the Yew is "the coffin of the vine", for it was from the wood of the Yew that wine-barrels were made. In Scotland, the Frasers of Lovat have the Yew as their 'plant badge'.

The Yew is by far the longest-lived tree in Europe, ever-green throughout the year. Because of its continuity and longevity, it is seen as a tree of everlasting life, sacred to various divinities and saints of death and regeneration. In Britain, Yews are commonly trees of churchyards, the burial-place of the dead. Ida's associated colour is dark greenish-brown, the colour of the tree's leaves. The under-bark and the resinous sap is blood-red, giving the phenomenon of the 'bleeding Yew', where a wounded tree oozes sap, as if bleeding. Such trees are held in great veneration.

Traditional European Yew-magic deals with the mysteries of life and death: Ida represents the magical staff or sliver of Yew, cut at the appropriate hour, which guards against all evil. Shakespeare's *Macbeth* tells of the "....slips of Yew, sliver'd in the Moon's eclipse" which is part of this tradition. As a time marker, it signifies the last day of the year, expressing the unity of opposites that occurs when the end of the old and the beginning of the new are present simultaneously.

## The Fifth Aicme

Ida is the final vowel of the 'conventional rubrics' of Ogham. The *Forfeadha* ('Overtrees') of the fifth *Aicme* are diphthongs, and in modern usage, they are ascribed various different meanings. Their correspondences are less well established than those of the first twenty characters, and they have a different form, being composed of complex strokes rather than the simple *Fleasc*.

**Eabhadh**
The first *ForFidh* of the fifth *Aicme* is the diphthong 'EA', Eabhadh. This is interpreted as the Aspen Tree (White Poplar, *Populus tremula*). If this is a correct ascription, then it has the same meaning as Edadh, the fourth *Fidh* of the fourth *Aicme* . In Brehon Law, this tree is *Crithach*. A contemporary view of this *Fidh* gives it a quite different interpretation, as Koad, with the phonetic value of 'K'. Colin Murray wrote that Koad signifies the unity of all eight festivals of the traditional year. He classified it as a Grove or Group rather than a tree. In this interpretation, it serves as a place for all hitherto separate things to be collected together. At such a point, all things become clear. The associated colours of Koad are all the 'forty shades of green'.

**Oir**
Oir has the phonetic value of 'Oi', and corresponds to the Spine or Spindle Tree (*Euonymus europaeus*), the eighth Royal Tree of the *Book of Ballymote*. In traditional craft, this

tree provided the spindles used in spinning thread. The Spindle grows best in the milder parts of the British Isles, but, during the nineteenth century, Spindle Trees were felled wholesale because the Black Bean Aphid was found to over-winter on them.

Contemporary interpretations of Oir view it as a *Fidh* of destiny, coming from the tree of the spindle of the Weaving Sisters who spin, weave, and cut the thread of life. It is also seen as a *Fidh* of childbirth, easing the passage of the baby from the womb into the world. Its associated colour is white. In his Golden Section Order teachings on the *Tree Alphabet*, Colin Murray viewed this *Fidh* as Tharan, with the phonetic value of 'Th', representing a sudden flash of illumination. Murray's interpretation thus links it with the thorn *Feadha*, hUath and Straif.

**Uinlleann**
The For*Fidh* called Uinlleann or Inlleann has the phonetic value of 'Ui'. According to The *Book of Ballymote*, this Ogham is associated with the Honeysuckle (*Lonicera caprifolium*). Medicinally, Honeysuckle is used for treating respiratory ailments, as Nicholas Culpeper tells us in his *Herbal* (1653), "Honeysuckles are cleansing, consuming and digesting, and therefore no way fit for inflammations ... it is a herb of Mercury, and appropriated to the lungs". Honeysuckle is a favourite food of goats, and its berries were formerly used to feed poultry.

Murray's interpretation calls this *Fidh* Peith, and gives it the phonetic value of 'P'. In the Golden Section Order teaching, Peith corresponds with the Guelder Rose or Snowball Tree (*Viburnum opulus*), a close relative of the Wayfaring Tree. It is not indigenous to Ireland. Here, Peith signifies an inner secret, a special dance or step that leads through the labyrinth of inner knowledge. This concept links it with the mystic *Geranos* or 'Crane Dance', performed upon labyrinths, and the crane-skin 'medicine bag' which ancient Celtic magicians are said to have used to carry their magical talismans and amulets. If this is an historically authentic interpretation, it may be connected with the Elder Futhark rune Perdhro (which does not appear, however in *Ogham Gall*, the Norse Younger Futhark rune-row used in early medieval Ireland).

## Ifin

According to the *Book of Ballymote*, the corresponding tree of this *Fidh* is Ifin, with the phonetic value of 'Io'. As a tree, Ifin is interpreted as the Gooseberry (*Ribes grossularia*), a cultivated species which may not be indigenous to the British Isles. The Welsh word for this fruit-bush is *Eirinen fair*, and in modern Irish, it is Spíonán. But an 'obsolete' Irish interpretation of Ifin is a vineyard (modern Irish, Fíonghort). This links Ifin with the next *Fidh*. Apart from being a fruit that is eaten, the Gooseberry has a medicinal function. In former times, the juice was said to cure all inflammations. The herbalist, Gerard, considered it a fine remedy for "hot, burning ague".

Again, the Golden Section Order correspondence is quite different from the *Book of Ballymote*'s Ogham Craobh. Here, Murray appears to take the Ogham Cnsaine (Consonantal Ogham) reading "PP in Ogham Io" (see Chapter 3). This is connected with the Beech tree (*Fagus sylvatica*), and rendered as Phagos, with the phonetic equivalent of 'Ph' or 'F'. The name of this tree in modern Irish is Feá, and the Welsh *ffawydden*. Murray refers it to the solidity of ancient wisdom, the cultural or physical foundation which must be in place before any construction can be started.

## Amhancholl

The final Ogham *Fidh* is a contentious character, being ascribed four different names: Péine, Amhancholl, Xi and Mír. It has the phonetic equivalent of 'Ae'. According to the *Book of*

*Ballymote*, it corresponds with Amhancholl, which is translated as Witch Hazel (*Hamamelis virginiana*). However, this cannot be a correct translation from a text written in 1391, because the Witch Hazel is a North American species that was introduced to the British Isles around the seventeenth century. What Amancholl means is thus open to question. As 'Ae', this *Fidh* takes the form of the grid of eight Ifins, which relates it to the previous *Fidh*.

The *Book of Ballymote* infers that this final *Fidh* is also Pine Ogham: "The figure resembles the hurdle of wrought twigs, or like a bier". According to one version of the story, the Pines that grew over the graves of Noísiu and Derdriu, buried on opposite banks of a loch, grew towards one another and finally their branches were entwined over the loch, making a natural hurdle. In *Cád Goddeu* we are told: "The Pine-Tree in the court, strong in battle, by me greatly exalted, in the presence of kings". In this form, Amhancholl's correspondence is taken as the evergreen Scots Pine (*Pinus sylvestris*) called in modern Irish, *Péine*, and in Welsh *Pinwydden*.

Symbolically, the Pine is the tree of illumination in the darkness, recalling the traditional technique of illumination using a chip of resinous pinewood, lit at one end. Contemporary esoteric interpretation sees this *Fidh* as the bringer of illumination, both on an intellectual and on a spiritual level. The Pine is the 'plant badge' of a number of Scottish clans, including Ferguson, Fletcher, Grant, MacAlpine, MacAulay, MacGregor and MacQuarne of Ulva.

This Ogham character has been subject to more speculative interpretation than most of them. As the twenty-fifth, it goes beyond the conventional 24-fold division of things customary in the Northern Tradition that include the 24 characters of the common Welsh Bardic *Coelbren*. Therefore, it is considered to stand outside the conventions of the other 24 Ogham *Feadha*, and even the other four For*feadha*. So, in addition to

14. The eternal flow of the waters, put into symbolic form by the fountain, signifies the cyclic nature of events that is implicit in Bardo-Druidic spirituality.

the correspondences with Witch Hazel and Pine, this *Fidh* has been given two further ascriptions - Xi, 'spirit', and Mór, 'the sea'. As Xi, this *Fidh* is seen as blue-green (or sea green) in colour. Murray's system saw this *Fidh* as symbolizing the hidden rhythms of the ebbing and flowing tides. According to his interpretation, Xi is at its most power-ful when the moon is full and the tide is high.

# Chapter 3

# Ogham Cryptography, Gall Ogham and the Gaelic Alphabet

## Alternative Forms

The *Book of Ballymote* describes a number of cryptic forms of Ogham. They include Oghaim Coll, where the *Feadha* are not composed of a series of strokes at all, but curved lines resembling the Roman letter 'C'. The *Book of Ballymote* describes them, thus:

"C - one C begins this Ogham fine.
CC - two C's right joined in O, you may combine in human speech with taste and show.
CCC - three C's well formed give U in equal rows.
CCCC - four C's make E fair seen by learning's eye.
CCCCC- five C's produce the ancient vowel I.
 C - two C's thus placed, the Irish Ifin Ogain.
   - two C's in a groove, UA in power retain.
   - one C thus placed, AO in order takes.
   - one C turned upside down OI bespeaks."

The 'Ogham of Consonants', a version of the consonantal Ogham called *Ogham Consaine*, is another cryptic system, based on letter transference. The *Book of Ballymote* tells us that " BH constitute A; FT rightly form U; NG bravely make I; LL of two L's make IA; PP in Ogham IO; DL invariably O; SC make E; MM from their backs give EA; BB pf two B's produce UA; and GG as directed".

## Alternative Correspondences

A significant way of creating Ogham letters is to use a series of things (in the widest sense) whose names begin with different letters. The first letter of each thing is then the Ogham *Fidh*. In the case of the trees and birds, the character of each species has a relationship with the inner meaning of its corresponding *Fidh*. But this may not be so clear in other instances. *Lin Ogham*, for instance, uses the place-names of pools of water, e.g. Banba (B), Luimneach (L), Febhal (F), Sinaind (S), Nearcnid (N). *Din Ogham* uses terms connected with a hill to describe the *Feadha*. *Naomh Ogham* employs the names of Irish saints: B is Brenaid; L, Laisreann; F, Finden; S, Sinchell, and N, Neasan. H is hAdamnan; D, Donnan; T, Tigheanach; C, Cronan, and Q, Qeran (Kieran). M is represented by Manchan; G, Guirgu; Ng, Ngeman; Cr, Crannan, and R, by Ruadhanachd. Finally, A is signified by An; O, Oena; U, Ultan; E, Eruan, and I, Ite.

'Battle Ogham' gives each letter to a weapon or other piece of military equipment, for example B corresponds with *Beanchor*, a horn, and numerous other objects and descriptions used in Ogham are described in the *Book of Ballymote*. The names of sciences, types of ship, herbs, meats, towns, etc. were used in medieval Ireland, and the principle is still open to modern uses.

## Alternative Numbers and Orders

The medieval cryptographers of Ireland devised all manner of ingenious alterations to *Ogham Craobh* to render it unintelligible to everyone who lacked the secret key. Some of these methods may have been derived from Roman, Byzantine or Scandinavian cryptography. *Feadha* can be encrypted by

15. Variant forms of Irish Ogham as recorded in the Book of Ballymote.

altering their form according to a fixed principle. The method called *Sluag Ogham* triples the number of strokes in each *Fidh*, creating The 'Ogham of the Multitudes'. 'The Ogham With an Additional One' adds an additional stroke to each *Fidh*, so that they number two to six, rather than one to five strokes for each *Aicme* (rubric). The 'Unison Ogham' writes the *Fidh* twice each time, BB for B, etc. For each *Fidh* in the Bonded Ogham, the character next to it is written also.

The Ogham 'Point Towards the Pit', reverses the direction of the strokes. The A *Aicme* reversed is in place of the B rubric, that is I for B and B for I; the M rubric reversed is in place of the H rubric; the B reversed in place of the A; and the H reversed in place of the M *Aicme*. 'End to End Ogham' brings together both ends of the Ogham 'alphabet' and reorganizes its inner order. In *Ogham Bricrenn*, 'The Ogham of Bricriu' (of the infamous 'feast'), the distance of a *Fidh* from the top of the 'alphabet' corresponds with the number of strokes written to form that single character, one for B and twenty for I.

The medieval Irish Oghamists reckoned the Rune-row of the *Younger Futhork* as *Gall Ogham*, 'The Ogham of the Foreigner'. Runic was introduced by Norwegian and Danish invaders in the tenth century. An antler found in excavations in Fishamble Street in Dublin in 1980 has a Norse inscription in these runes. There is also a wooden sliver from the same district of Norse Dublin bearing the whole 16-Rune row. In the *Book of Ballymote*, this Rune row is in a different order than the standard Futhork. The Runes are remembered in modern Irish, where the word *Ogham* means the ancient alphabet, but words for people who deal with writing are all based on the root Rún. A 'secretary' is Rúna", whilst a 'private secretary' is Rúncléireac, literally, 'rune-clerk'. By the time that the Runes were in everyday use in Dublin a thousand years ago, the Oghams were no longer used for everyday writing.

However, even when they were no longer apparent, the Oghams flourished among scholars and poets as secret writing and signs. Medieval Oghamists encrypted names and words by changing the letter-order either within the Ogham-row or in the word itself. In the 'Ogham of Order', the word is arranged in the order that its *Feadha* have in the 'alphabet'. In *Ogham Deginach*, 'The Final Ogham', the last letter of the name of a *Fidh* is used instead of the first, S for Luis etc. 'The Ogham of Extraordinary Disturbance' puts the first letter of every *Aicme* in place of the B *Aicme*; the second letters for the second *Aicme*, and so on through the whole Ogham-row of 25 *Feadha*.

Some cryptic Oghams are named after the shape they take. One is The Adder in the Heath, a strange name for snakeless Ireland, indicating that this version may have related to a cryptographic system with the same name from elsewhere, as may have the system called The Adder [Coiled] Around [Its] Head. The *Book of Ballymote* tells us, "to write the first letter of the name in the middle of the Craobh (line of *Feadha*), and to write the name from it in direct order to the end of the line, and in reversed order to the beginning; so that it is the same thing that is written at the beginning and at the end of the line, that is, the end of the name is what is on either [end] of it...With equal correctness it is to be read down and up, and it is from the middle the name is read, for the first letter of the name is there." In Ogham *Adlen Fid*, the 'Struggle of the Chase' links two names. The first half of the first name is written, then the first half of the second. They are followed by the end of the first name, and then the end of the second.

## Spatial Disposition

Among the 150 ancient Irish Oghams are 'The Wall-Fern Ogham'; 'The Piercing Ogham'; 'Fionn's Tooth-like Ogham'; *Fege Finn* ('Fionn's Window'); 'Fionn's Wheel'; and 'Fionn's Shield', which is a version of *Ogham Airenach*, 'Shield-

Ogham'). The final four forms of are named after the legendary Irish hero Fionn Mac Cumhaill, whose name is often Anglicized to Finn McCool. Son-in-law of King Cormac Mac Art, Fionn was the commander of the army known as the *Fianna Erenn*. According to the *Annals of Tighernach*, he was killed in the year 284 CE. Fionn's Oghams are based on their position on concentric circles or squares within a circular or square framework. Their disposition relates them to corresponding aspects of traditional cosmology, such as the directions, times of day, or spiritual states of being (see *Appendix* 6 for parallels).

The Ogham of 'Fionn's Window' and 'Fionn's Shield' is related to the technique called *Luaithrindi*. This is a magical binding-knot or optical illusion painted on a shield. One appeared on the shield of the hero Cuchulainn, who demanded that his shield-maker should create an engraving unlike all others. Such patterns often created optical illusions that had the function of distracting the opponent in combat.

The use of complementary colours in interlace patterns, such as those in the *Lindisfarne Gospels*, where red and blue are used together, was known to produce a dazzling effect. The tesselated patterns, known from Celtic and Hiberno-Saxon artwork, if painted in strongly contrasting colours, also have this effect. The Ogham colours in themselves would also spell out a message to those who could read it.

### Pictorial and Literary Oghams

Because each *Aicme* of the *Ogham Craobh* denotes the *Feadha* by strokes numbering between one and five, it is possible to denote the *Feadha* by groups of other things. This gives the possibility of spelling words by sequences of pictures, or by description. There are many recorded Oghams of this kind, denoting only the first four rubrics of *Craobh Ogham*. As an illustration of the principle, there is the *Faun*

*Ogham*. For the *Aicme* of B, a buck (*Dam*) is depicted, one for the first *Fidh*, two for the second, and so on, until N is represented by five bucks. The second *Aicme*, beginning with H, is represented by one to five does (*Elit*). The third *Aicme*, beginning M, has a faun (*Iarnu*), whilst the fourth *Aicme*, beginning with A, has a 'sucking calf' (*Laeg*).

The *Arms Ogham* operates on exactly the same principle. A dart (*Gai*) stands for the rubric beginning B; a shield (Sciath) for H; a broadsword (*Claidim*) for M; and a 'good or red-pointed sword' (*Colg*) for the fourth *Aicme*, beginning with A. Human Ogham (*Daen Ogham*) is the same. One to five men or champions stand for the first five *Feadha*; women or clergymen for the next five, H to Q; youths for the M to R rubric; and sons or slaves for the vowels. For the four rubrics of Con Ogham (*Dog Ogham*), there are one to five of each of the following: collared hounds, greyhounds, pups and lapdogs. Ox Ogham (*Damh Ogham*) uses bulls, oxen, a yearling and a herd-bull, whilst *Cow Ogham* (*Bo Ogham*) has 'milch-cows', 'strippers', 'fatlings' and cows with calves.

The possibilities of interconnection and symbolic allusion are limitless. In former times, by such means, initiates could communicate with one another simply by mentioning the animals, birds, weapons, etc. that corresponded with the letters. Unsuspecting listeners had no idea of what they meant. The scope in symbolic prose and poetry of this sort of esoteric correspondence is immense. Any piece of literature can contain hidden messages based upon the names of things and places.

Secret visual communication was also possible when Ogham was used as a form of semaphore or sign-language. These systems employed the fingers to represent the characters. It may be surmised that Ogham itself originated with these hand-signs. Coir Ogham transmits messages by laying fingers around the foot or shinbone. They are laid, one to five, across the shinbone from the right for the *Aicme* of B; on the left side for H to Q; diagonally for M to R; and straight across for the vowels. *Bar Ogham* is a hand-sign language which used the fingers of one hand laid across the other one to make standard or cryptic Ogham characters. In *Sron Ogham*, the fingers are laid across the central stem of the nose in the same way as for *Coir Ogham*.

## Colour Ogham

Another visual form of Ogham is *Muc Ogham* (Colour Ogham), which ascribes a colour to each *Fidh*. In Colour Ogham, B is expressed by Ban, white; Luis, *Liath*, grey; F, *Flann*, crimson; S by *Sodath*, 'bright', and N by *Necht*, 'clear'. The colour of Huath is also called *Huath*, 'terrible'; D is *Dubh*, black; T, *Temen*, grey-green or dark grey; Coll, *Cron*, brown; and Q, *Quiar*, 'mousey'. The next *Aicme* begins with the multi-coloured *Mbracht*, M, followed by Gort, *Gorm*, blue, and *Nglas*, Ng, glass-green. Straif is represented by *Sorcha*, 'bright-coloured', and Ruis by *Ruadh*, bright red. The fourth *Aicme* is A, Alad, black-and-white; O, *Odhar*, brownish black; *Usgdha*, U, purple; E, *Erc*, 'fox-red'; and finally *Irfind*, I, brilliant white.

For contemporary users, Colour Ogham is difficult to use because the ancient Irish terminology of colours operates according to quite different principles of perception than are used to-day. *Muc Ogham* provides richly symbolic possibilities to encode written meanings into artwork, abstract patterns, ornament, heraldry, fabrics, clothing, rites and ceremonies.

Typically, the standard form of *Colour Ogham* was not the only one. Swine Ogham is based on the colours of swine, as the *Book of Ballymote* tells us: "White - any shade of fairness; grey - any shade of grey; black, brown, ultra-grey, etc." There is also "A vessel curved underneath, a dismal habitation, worthless people, speckled, the light green colour, red; light

16. According to contemporary Druidic teachings, the trilithon signifies the three consonantal groups of Oghams, with the ground between the stones representing the vowels.

doe colour, red doe colour, half-white or greyish-white, black, variegated....".

## Obscure Ogham Formulae

Historically, the magical use of Ogham seems to have employed certain formulae whose nature is obscure. An inscription of a magical nature is known from a stone at Glenfahan, where the letters "LMCBDV" are cut. Another cryptic inscription, "MTBCML" appears on an amber bead from Ennis, formerly used as a cure for sore eyes, and to ensure safe births. It was last used by a certain Mr Finerty, from whom it was acquired by J.H. Greaves, a jeweller from Cork. He sold it to Lord Londesborough, who gave it to the British Museum.

In 1888, at a place called Biere, near Quedlinburg, Saxony, Germany, a schoolmaster called Rabe reported finding a large number of limestone tablets. There were 1200 specimens in all. They were carved with representations of hammers, axes, shields, swords, javelins, spearheads, arrows and bows. What made them most interesting was the Ogham inscriptions that accompanied the images. Dr Gustav Brecht identified the carvings as dating from the Merovingian period (5th - 8th centuries CE). Along with the obvious Oghams were other cryptic symbols resembling 'tent runes' and numerical Oghams.

The inscriptions were rather enigmatic. For example, an image of a horn had Ogham *Feadha* interpreted as "TOTOTUMT"; an axe was accompanied by "TODAL"; a bird by "CLATF"; a bow and arrow by "TODLAH", and a bow by "TOTADA". If they are genuinely ancient, the Biere stones may have some connection with the activities of those Irish Christian missionaries who brought book learning and monastic life to parts of central Europe. Ogham was certainly used at the monastery of St Gall at St Gallen in modern

Switzerland, and it is likely that it found its way to other Celtic-founded religious houses, too. The Biere Stones were accepted as genuine by R.A.S.Macalister, who commented in his *Studies in Irish Epigraphy*, that they seemed to settle, once and for all, the use of Ogham as a medium of magic.

## The Gaeílge/Gaelic Aíbítír

Unlike the Oghams and Coelbrens, the Irish and Scottish *Aibítir* (alphabet) is actually a true *alphabet*, derived directly from Graeco-Roman sources. It is related to Ogham in that all but two *Litir* (letters or characters) correspond with a tree. The two characters that do not, mean 'fire' and 'garden'. The Gaelic alphabet has seventeen full characters, and although there appears to be an eighteenth *Litir*, equivalent to the Roman letter 'H', it is actually ranked as an accent and not a character in its own right.

The Gaelic *Aibítir* has its letters in the same order as the Roman alphabet. It is quite different from the order of the Oghams or the Runes. But, as in the case of Ogham, most of the characters of the Gaelic *Aibítir* have esoteric correspondences with specific trees. Unlike Ogham, however, the first letter of the Gaelic *Aibítir* is called Fhalm, the Elm tree, with the phonetic value of A. Next comes Beath, the Birch tree, phonetically B. This is equivalent to the first *Fidh* of the Oghams. The third letter is Calltuinn, the Hazel tree, C. This is followed by Doir, the Oak tree, the letter D. The fifth *Litir* of the *Aibítir* is called Eubh, the Aspen tree, the character standing for the phonetic E. The sixth is Fearn, the Alder tree, F.

*Litir* number seven is not called after a tree. It is Gart, meaning 'garden' or 'vineyard'. The next letter resumes the tree correspondence, being Iubhar, the Yew tree, phonetically I. The Yew is followed by Luis, the letter L, equivalent to the Quicken or Rowan tree. Muin, the Vine, has the value of the letter M. Next is N, Nuin, the Ash tree. The twelfth letter of the *Aibítir* stands for the letter O, Oir, the Furze. Beith-bhog, the Poplar tree, stands for the letter P. There is no 'Q' in the *Aibítir*, and Beith-bhog is followed by the letter R, Ruis, the Alder tree. The fifteenth *Litir* is the letter S, Suil, the Willow tree. The sixteenth character is not a tree. Its name is Teine, which means Fire, and signifies the letter T. The final character of the Gaelic *Aibítir* is, Uhr, the letter U. Like Iubhar, this also stands for the Yew Tree.

As with the Greek and Hebrew alphabets, each Litir corresponds with a number. The first letter, Fhalm, is also the number, one; Beath, two; Calltuinn, three. Doir, the fourth character, has the value, four; Eubh is five; and Fearn, six. Number seven is Gart, followed by Iubhar, eight. Ninth is number nine, Luis, and tenth is Muin, with a value of 10. This is followed by the Ash-tree letter, Nuin, number 11. Twelfth is number 12, Oir. Number 13 is Beith-bhog, then number 14, Ruis. Fifteenth and equivalent to the number 15, is the character called Suil, the Willow-letter. Number 16 is Teine, the fire-character, and finally, Uhr completes the numbers as 17.

The letters of the Gaelic *Aibítir* do not have exactly the same meaning as the Ogham *Feadha*. Neither thorn tree, Black or White, appear. Neither the Apple, nor the Spindle nor Ivy. The Yew tree, however, is represented twice, by the Iubhar and Uhr, the letters I and U. In Ogham, the *Fidh* equivalent to U, Up, corresponds with the Heather. Also, in the Gaelic *Aibítir*, the Elm Tree, Fhailm, is the primary character, not the Birch Tree Beath.

Describing 'The Divisions of Ogham' in the *Book of Ballymote*, Elm is noted as the first Royal (Chieftain) Tree. As this is the first Litir of the Gaelic *Aibítir*, this posits an ancient connection between the Ogham trees and this alphabet. The use of Fhailm as the first letter may reflect the Northern

*17. (p.50) The Gaelic Aibitir, Y prif un awgrym ar bymtheg the 'sixteen primary symbols', the Awen and other Northern Tradition alphabets Abcedilros and Futhork.*

Tradition myth that the first woman, Embla, was fashioned from an Elm tree. As woman is the fount of all human life, this would be most appropriate. Teine has its more logical ascription of 'fire', unlike the corresponding Ogham *Fidh*, which represents the Holly Tree. Perhaps because it is shorter, and more limited, or younger that Ogham, the Gaelic *Aibítir* is more coherent, possessing no awkward correspondences or herbal ascriptions that disrupt consistency. Although little used today symbolically, the Gaelic *Aibítir* remains a very useful system when employed as a means of divination or for other esoteric purposes.

# Chapter 4
# Deities of the Sacred Forest

In Pagan times, the Celtic veneration of trees was expressed sometimes in the form of gods and goddesses. Some were general deities of sacred woods or groves, whilst others were the gods of individual types of trees. The god Callirius, for example, worshipped in Roman times at Colchester, appears to be a Hazel-god, (from Coll). The god Vernostonus, from Ebchester, has a name that is thought to mean 'Alder Tree' (Fearn), whilst a god called Deus Fagus (*The God of the Beech*) was venerated in the French Pyrenees. The Gaulish god Alisanos may have been a god of the Rowan tree (Luis), though this interpretation is less certain. The god Esus, otherwise called Esunertus or Esugenus appears on the memorial called the Pillar of the Nautae of Paris, which was dedicated to Jupiter in the year 13 BCE. Here, he is depicted with an axe in his hand, pruning or cutting a tree. The Bern Scholiasts of Lucan tell that human sacrifices were made to Esus: Men were hanged on trees and stabbed at the same time so that omens could be read from the way that they bled.

Before the Romans influenced them to build temples, the Pagan Celts worshipped in holy groves of trees. Called *nemeton*, they were 'clearings open to the sky', special places in woodland, entered only by priests and priestesses. In his *Pharsalia*, Lucan tells of the Gaulish Druids who lived in deep groves and remote uninhabited woods. His Scholiast added that "They worship the gods in the woods without using temples". Much later, Christian prohibitions of the time of Charlemagne (c. 800 CE) condemned the Pagan ceremonies in the woodlands, called *Nimidas*, and the Yries, 'Pagan Trackways' that linked the sacred places of the forest. The *Silva Gadelica* tells how many sacred places of the Gaels were once groves of Hazel trees.

Many former Celtic *nemeton* sites are known to-day. An old Irish name for a sacred wood is *Fidnemet*, and in France, the name of the city of Nanterre recalls the Celtic name 'Nemetodunum'. In England, there are the former 'Vernemeton', 'the especially sacred grove', and in southern Scotland, 'Medionemeton', 'the central grove'. Villages in Devon called Nympton also recall Celtic groves. Like the later temples, groves were set up or dedicated to specific deities. Dio Cassius reports that the Britons worshipped in groves where they sacrificed to Andraste, goddess of victory (she may be a version of Adrasteia, equivalent to the Greek Nemesis). A Gallo-Roman altar from Vaison in Vaucluse in the south of France, commemorates the establishment of a *nemeton* in honour of the goddess Belesama, who was also worshipped in Britain as the goddess of the River Mersey.

The goddess Nemetona (The Goddess of the Holy Grove), was worshipped at the great healing water shrine of Aquae Sulis (Bath) as well as Altripp, Mainz and Trier in Germany. She was the goddess of the grove-named Nemetes tribe in the Rhine valley. In Romanized lands, Nemetona was the consort of Mars Rigonemetis, whose name means, 'The King of the Holy Grove'. Rigonemetis was also worshipped at a shrine at Nettleham near Lincoln, whilst the goddess Arnemetia was another deity of holy groves, worshipped at the healing springs of Buxton in the modern Derbyshire. Another name for a holy forest is *Lucus*, as in the holy forest of the tree- and spring deity, Burmanus, *Lucus Burmani*, around Cervo in Liguria, Italy. From these examples, it is clear that tree-

*18. (p,53) The Cosmic Axis that links the lower Cylch (circle) or world of Annwn with this present middleworld (Abred) and the upper worlds of Gwynvyd and Ceugant.*

deities were a significant element in ancient Celtic spirituality.

## Single Trees

A lone holy tree known as *bile* grew at every holy place of inauguration of Celtic nobility. The French place-name Billom comes from the Celtic Biliomagus, 'the plain of the sacred tree[1]. Offerings and the remains of rites and ceremonies were hung in the branches of *bile* trees. Sometimes, holy trees were tended and altered to give them symbolic shapes, such as Cross Trees, Dancing Trees and the Trained Lindens of mainland Europe. There was even an ancient Celtic god called Olludius, whose name means 'Great Tree'. Remains of his worship have been found at Custom Scrubs in Gloucestershire, England and at Antibes in the south of France. Olludius is shown as a *genius loci*, dressed in a short tunic with a cloak and hood.

There were five notable venerable trees in ancient Ireland, described in the *Rennes Dindsenchas*. One tree stood for each province. They were the trees of Ross, Mugna, Tortu, Datha and Uisnech. The branching Ash tree of Uisnech was at the omphalos of the island. It grew alongside the Stone of Division, the navel of Ireland. Mugna's tree was an evergreen Oak that bore three varieties of fruit. In addition to acorns, it produced apples and nuts, perhaps from grafted branches.

*Druim Suithe*, a medieval Irish poem about the oracular tree of Leinster, the Tree of Ross, reveals the many layers of meaning that the Celtic Bards saw in such trees:

> "Tree of Ross:
> A king's wheel,
> A prince's right,
> A wave's noise,
> Best of creatures:
> A straight, firm tree.

85

19. Ogham's universal nature readily lends it to the creation of artistic and meaningful patterns. Like other Celtic art, this is a proper ornamental antidote to meaningless modernist abstraction.

A firm, strong god,
Door of Heaven,
Strength of a building,
The good of a crew,
A word-pure man,
Full-great bounty,
The Trinity's mighty one,
A measure's hours,
A mother's god,
Mary's Son,
A fruitful sea
Beauty's honour,
A mind's lord,
Diadem of angels,
Shout of the world,
Banba's renown,
Might of Victory,
Judgement of origin,
Judicial doom,
Faggot of sages,
Noblest of trees,
Glory of Leinster,
Dearest of bushes,
A bear's defence,
Vigour of life,
Spell of knowledge,
Tree of Ross."

Symbolic trees also feature in Welsh poetry. *The Black Book of Carmarthen*, written around 1250, contains a poem beginning "Gwyn y bid hi y vedwen in diffrin Guy" ("Blessed be the Birch in the Wye Valley"). Each stanza of the poem tells of a notable Birch tree that will witness certain results of a battle in Ardudwy. Three Birches are named: that in the Valley of the Wye; the Birch tree of Pumlumon; and the Birch on top of Difythwy. Another poem in *The Black Book* is called *Afallennau* (usually translated as *Merlin's Apple Trees*). Each stanza begins with *afallen*, and, like the Birches, refers to trees in different locations. In it is the story of how Merlin hides in an Apple tree to escape the wrath of King Rhydderch. Merlin's trees include Apples that grow "on the edge"; "beyond the Rhun"; "in Llanerch"; "in a nook in Argoedydd"; "on the river bank"; "in grounds with various kinds of tree"; and the Apple "with Foxglove-pink flowers that grows secretly in the Forest of Caledon".

As a symbol of stability and living continuity, the Celtic battle-standard was the oak tree. The Welsh archers who fought with the English army at Agincourt in 1415 carried images of Merlin's Oak from Carmarthen, reflecting the epithet "might of victory". In the Irish poem, *The Battle of Moyragh* the Bard John O'Donovan tells us of the battle-standard of O'Loughlin:

> In O'Loughlin's camp was visible a fair satin sheet
> To be at the head of each battle to defend in battle-field.
> An ancient fruit-bearing oak, defended by a chieftain
>    justly,
> And an anchor blue, with folds of a golden cable".

The Oak tree is the heraldic emblem of the O'Connors to this day. It is also the 'plant badge' of clans Anderson, Buchannan, Cameron, MacEwen, Kennedy and Stewart. The *Royal Oak* was long a symbol of monarchist loyalty in Great Britain. One of the epithets of the Tree of Ross is "judicial doom". This is a reference to the execution of criminals and prisoners by hanging on trees. In former times in the Scottish highlands were trees upon which the clan chieftains hanged their enemies. This was in exercise of their powers of "pit and gallows", the legal right to drown women in a pit and to hang men on the tree. Known as *Dool-trees* or *Grief Trees*, they grew on small hillocks which were known consequently as Gallows Hills.

## Sacred Forests and Their Destroyers

In Pagan times, certain Celtic forests were held in reverence. The greatest of them were the Breton forests of Brocéliande and Morrois and the Scottish Wood of Caledon. Sadly, they are shadows of their former glory, for centuries of deforestation have reduced them to small remnants. In Brittany, the last remains of Brocéliande are the Forêt de Huelgoat and the Forêt de Paimpont. Also surviving are the twin mystic woods called Coat-an-Hay and Coat-an-Noz, The 'Day Wood' and 'Night Wood'. In Scotland, the forest known as The Wood of Caledon was once continuous from Glen Coe to Braemar and from Glen Lyon to Glen Affric. According to tradition, it was destroyed by a monster called *Muime*, which was brought from Scandinavia to fly over the forest and burn it down.

In reality, the Wood of Caledon was extensively cut and burnt by Scottish woodsmen between the ninth and twelfth centuries. By then, the former Pagan veneration of forests had been seriously weakened by the Christian religion. Clansmen set large tracts of woodland on fire to kill members of other clans, and to exterminate the wolves and other wild beasts that lived there. In later years, further parts of the forest fell to the ship-builders and was burnt in the forges of iron-masters. In the twentieth century, the national emergencies of the two world wars were the excuse for yet further destruction.

To-day, the only significant remnant of this splendid Caledonian forest is the Black Wood of Rannoch at Loch Tulla. As men of the trees, the Bards were not unaware of the unfolding ecological disaster with the deforestation of Brittany, Wales, Scotland and Ireland. The Irish Bard, Aodhagan O Rathaille lamented, "Woe, your woods are withering away". In Wales, the Valley sides were deforested for fuel and the animals exterminated to make way for iron works. As an anonymous sixteenth century Welsh Bard wrote of the destruction of Glyn Cynon Wood by English iron-

20. The mystery of smithcraft, as expressed in the northern European legend of Wayland, demonstrates the ambivalent nature of creation that also involves destruction.

workers, "There was nothing ever more disastrous than the cutting of Glyn Cynon". Once the forests were felled, men began to dig out fossil fuel from coal mines to fuel the furnaces of Wales and Scotland. Where there was little or no coal, as in Ireland, there was no 'industrial revolution'.

From Roman times onward, military and spiritual conquerors had been particularly intent on destroying Celtic sacred groves, which they saw as centres of native loyalty. During his Gallic wars in the middle of the first century BCE, Julius Caesar destroyed a *nemeton* near Marseille that contained trees that had been carved into the images of goddesses and gods. A century later, during his persecution of British Druidry, the Roman general Suetonius Paulinus desecrated and destroyed the groves on the holy isle of Anglesey. In 452 CE, the Christian Council of Arles banned the veneration of trees, springs and stones in southern France. The Councils of Tours in 567 CE, and Nantes in 568, extended the prohibitions in the north of France and in Brittany. Christian missionaries like St Martin of Tours and St Patrick cut down Pagan holy trees in France and Ireland respectively. Early in the eleventh century, the Christian Irish *Ard Rí*, Brian Boru, took a month to cut down and burn the sacred grove of the Northmen's god, Thor, near Dublin. And in 1351, Johannes, Grand Master of the Teutonic Knights, caused the cutting-down of the holy Oak tree at Romove in East Prussia.

Because Celtic Christianity was in direct continuity with Celtic Paganism, churches were built on traditional holy places, which were Pagan. Although some missionaries, like St Martin of Tours, made it a matter of principle to cut down Pagan holy trees, it is probable that in many cases they remained when the *Comraich* was re-dedicated to the new religion. Sometimes, the presence of Pagan trees has been recorded in place-names. According to his biographer, Rhygyfarch, St David was educated at a monastery in west Wales at Yr Henllwyn 'The Old Bush', called in Latin *Vetus*

*Rubus*. Churches are sometimes named after trees. The church after which the town of Killarney in Ireland is named is the 'church of the Blackthorn', Cill Airne. To-day, ancient churchyards frequently contain venerable and venerated trees, especially ancient Yews.

## Trees of Memory and Inspiration

As holders of ancestral heritage, the Celtic Bards were the recounters of history and genealogy. They were the writers of epitaphs and eulogies, and oversaw the rites of burial of notable people, who, as in the words of the Bard Dafydd ap Gwilym (1340-1400), "did well in their lives". The Bards planted trees on graves and at special locations to commemorate important events. An ancient Yew in the ruins of Strata Florida Abbey in Dyfed was planted to mark the grave of Dafydd ap Gwilym. It is a living monument to the great Bard, a tree of memory. One of the reputed graves of the wizard Merlin in Brittany, near Paimpont, is marked by a Holly tree. The tradition of record is made overt in the Irish story of the Apple and Yew that grew on the grave of Bailé MacBuain and Aillinn. After seven years, we are told, the Bards cut the trees and made Poets' Tablets from them. "If poets' verses be but stories", wrote St Colum Cille, "So be food and raiment stories; So be all the world a story. So is man of dust a story".

Isolated rows of thickly-planted trees in Scotland, called *Bell Trees* (c.f. Bile) are held in great regard, for they commemorate ancestors of families and clans. Sometimes, the very fortunes of families are bound up with the fate of individual trees, such as "the Oak of fate from the wood". For example, the great tree growing at Howth Castle in Ireland was linked with the St Lawrence family, the Earls of Howth. We find the same tradition in Great Britain. In Scotland, at Dalhousie Castle, near Edinburgh, grew the Edgewell Tree. The destiny of the Edgewell family was said to depend upon the condition of this tree. Another famed Scottish tree, the Oak of Errol, bore a Mistletoe plant whose fate was bound up with the Hays of Errol in the Carse of Gowrie. In his book, *Forest Folklore* (1928), Alexander Porteous quotes a member of the Hays, writing of the *Geassa* in 1822: "the duration of the family of Hay was said to be united with its existence .... the two most unlucky deeds which could be done by one of the name of Hay was, to kill a white falcon, and to cut down a limb from the Oak of Errol". In England, it was said that the Fulford family, living near the Cornwall-Devon border, held their lands on condition that once a year they dined upon the platform in the branches of the great Oak at Dunsford, and held a dance there for their tenants.

Similarly, the state of Merlin's Oak in Carmarthen, Pembrokeshire, west Wales, was said to reflect the condition of the town. This was a very famous tree, for the Welsh archers who gave the strategic advantage to the King of England's army at the Battle of Agincourt in 1415 carried images of Merlin's Oak for luck. In the nineteenth century, Merlin's Oak was killed deliberately by a religious fanatic who disapproved of the crowds that congregated there, day and night. For many years afterwards, the Oak's lifeless bole stood in the street, in latter times propped up by concrete and iron. Sadly, no attempt was made to plant a new tree, and eventually, to make room for more traffic, the dead trunk was transported to the museum. This was ironic, considering the tradition that the spirit of the town was embodied in Merlin's living tree: "When Merlin's Oak shall tumble down, Then shall fall Carmarthen town."

In 1745, the Jacobite Bard Alasdair Macdonald planted an oak at Dalilea House at Moidart in Scotland, in celebration of the return of 'Bonnie Prince Charlie' in his attempt to regain the throne for the Stuarts. In the next century, whole plantations were made on estates all over Scotland to commemorate the victory of the British Army over Napoleon at the Battle of Waterloo. The shapes and spatial relationship of

21.Merlin, the archetypal Celtic wise-but-wild man who lives at the boundaries of the human, animal and plant realms.

plantations in the landscape reproduced the disposition of the military units in the battle. They still exist on the promontory at the eastern entrance to the Kyles of Bute at Loch Striven, and as the Glenearn Woods by the Bridge of Earn in Tayside. The custom was continued in 1948, when a wood in the shape of a crown was planted at Rothesay on the Isle of Bute to celebrate the birth of the heir to the throne of the United Kingdom, Prince Charles.

Trees are living beings whose ensoulment makes them perfect media through which we can draw inspiration. The intimate relationship between Bards and trees is evident throughout history. The mad Merlin in his Apple tree, the Oghams, the Tablets of the Poets and "the wattles and the branches" of Welsh poetry are among the many manifestations. Thus, specific trees are associated with places of learning. In 1458, William Waynflete, Bishop of Winchester, founded Magdalen College at Oxford. It was located in the shadow of the Great Oak, which lived until 1788. The Caerwys Tree in north Wales is actually an authentic Bardic tree of inspiration. The present tree is a Sycamore, planted in the mid-twentieth century to replace the earlier one, which had perished. From 1568, when Queen Elizabeth I authorized the first official *Eisteddfod* (Bardic session) at Caerwys, competing Bards sat around the base of the tree to compose, then walked across the road to perform their new poems at the *Eisteddfod* hall.

## Fruit-Bearing Trees

Although they destroyed Pagan holy trees and groves, some Celtic Christians were also planters. In sixth-century CE Brittany, the *Liber Landavensis* records that the British monks Teilo and Samson "planted a great grove of fruit-bearing trees, to the extent of three miles, from Dól as far as Cai." To this day, St Teilo is the patron of apple-trees. In former times in Wales, all trees growing on land dedicated to St Beuno were considered sacred, and were never cut or damaged in any way. In the medieval text called *The Essentials of a Physician*, the physicians of Myddfai deemed it necessary that a medical practitioner should have "A garden of trees and herbs, where such herbs, shrubs and trees, as do not everywhere grow naturally, may be kept cultivated, and where foreign trees and plants, which require shelter and culture before they will thrive in Wales, may be grown".

The present veneration of apple-orchards by many people is a continuation of the ancient respect for sacred groves. In Herefordshire, it was the custom that if a man wanted to take over a piece of common land, he must first plant an apple tree there. From medieval times, the *Privileges* of the Free Miners of the Forest of Dean, Cornwall and elsewhere have permitted them to prospect for, and extract coal and minerals in areas where they were plentiful. Their Royal Charters, which have precedents in ancient Welsh law, give the Free Miners the right to dig on any land, with three exceptions. They may not dig up the Queen's Highway, consecrated churchyards, or orchards of fruit-bearing trees.

Writing in *The Folklore of Herefordshire* (1912), Ella Mary Leather comments, "The apple is our Herefordshire tree *par excellence*; the old labourers look upon the destruction of an orchard almost as an act of sacrilege, and they say that if an orchard be cut down to plant a hopyard, it will never pay the cost of cultivation." The tradition continues in many parts of England and Wales of wassailing the orchards, often on Twelfth Night (January 6), when offerings of bread and cider or ale are made to apple trees. Cider may be poured over the roots, shotguns are fired three times through the branches, fireworks and party poppers are let off, drums are beaten, traditional wassail songs are sung, and the health of the trees drunk in cider and other strong beverages.

## Renewal

Like all living things, trees have a limited life, so when a notable tree dies it is customary to plant a new one in its place. The new tree should be grown from a cutting of the old one, or, if this is not possible, from a seedling of its fruit. In this way, the old tree is reborn in its original location, and continuity can be possible over thousands of years. But when this principle is not understood, and the old, dead, tree is preserved as a relic, then the opportunity to plant anew is lost. Eventually, the remains of the dead tree will disintegrate with time, or be removed. Then the place ceases to be special. This happened at Carmarthen in west Wales, where Merlin's Oak was not replaced by a new one. However, all is not lost, for the tradition does continue in many places, such as at Caerwys. At Lillington, near Leamington Spa, one of the places reputed to be the centre of England, grew a tree called 'The Midland Oak'. When it died in 1982, a new tree was planted to replace it. Similarly, the 'Arbour Tree', a flag-bedecked Poplar at Aston-upon-Clun in Shropshire, was replanted in the mid-1990s. Whenever such a notable old tree perishes, it is necessary that local people keep up the tradition, and plant another for the enjoyment of future generations.

## 'Green Men': Men and Women of the Trees

The name *Green Man*, describing foliated faces in medieval churches, was first used as recently as 1939 by Lady Raglan in an article in the journal *Folklore*. It is used almost universally to-day to describe any face surrounded by leaves in various ways or even formed entirely of leaves. They appear as building ornament, sacred or secular, as well as in medieval manuscripts. Such images of human faces in foliage can be traced back into Celto-Roman times. They appear to represent several different mythic and legendary beings. The Gaulish god Erriapus, who is known best from the Garonne

22. The Green Man, whose mask appears in medieval churches throughout western Europe, is a significant figure in contemporary Paganism.

region of France, is depicted on an altar from Saint-Beat as a head emerging from foliage. 'Leaf masks' also appeared in Roman art during the first century CE. A foliated face, seemingly a water-being, perhaps the god Neptune, forms the centrepiece of the great silver dish dated to the mid-fourth century CE, found with other Roman remains at Mildenhall in Suffolk.

A fragment of Roman masonry from a demolished second century Gallo-Roman temple seems to have played a significant role in the development of the architectural 'green man'. It was incorporated into the sixth-century CE cathedral at Trier in the Rhineland. It bore a foliated 'leaf mask' which may have influenced church builders in the 'Romanesque' style elsewhere, becoming a widespread ornamental motif. Fragments of the medieval tomb of St Frideswide in Oxford Cathedral show her face amid foliage. These images refer to the story of how she hid in the forest when hunted by an unwelcome suitor. Other images show beings with branches or leaves emanating from nostrils or mouth, or forming the hair or beard. This type of medieval 'Green Man' was the subject of an exhaustive study by Kathleen Basford published in 1978, titled *The Green Man*.

The 'Wild Man' or 'Woodwose' was a popular character in medieval pageants, *Pas d'Armes*, tournaments and carnivals, and appears to-day at *Fasnacht* (Shrovetide) and in autumnal festivals in various parts of south Germany, Switzerland and the Tyrol. The inventory of the properties for the Feast of the Nativity at Otford in Kent in 1348 includes "XII wildmen's heads" (masks). The tournament called the *Pas d'Armes de la Sauvage Dame*, held in Ghent (Flanders) in 1469, was opened by two 'Wild Men' with trumpets and two others, leading richly-caparisoned horses on which rode two 'Wild Ladies', carrying the prizes for the victor. In his *Garland of Laurel*, the English Poet Laureate John Skelton (c1460-1528), wrote of "Diana in the leaves green".

In the Alpine region, Wild Men and Women are said to symbolize the spirit of free, natural life, bringing strength, health and fertility. Guisers dressed as 'Wild Men' and 'Wild Women' are recorded from the Schempartlauf in Nuremberg in 1470, 1539 and the eighteenth century. The wild people of Älplerchilbi in Switzerland are recorded as far back as 1624. In Great Britain in the reign of King James VI/I, the men whose job it was to let off fireworks at celebrations were called 'Green Men'. *The Seven Champions of Christendom* has the line, "Have you any squibs, any green-men in your shows?".

The story of *Orson and Valentine* appears first in a French romance of 1489. It tells of twin brothers, born in a wood at Orleans and separated at birth when Orson is carried off by a she-bear. The bear raises him with her cubs, and he becomes a wild man, whilst Valentine is raised as a nobleman. The play takes place when they meet, years later, and Orson is captured during a hunt. Later, Orson overthrows the Pagan Green Knight and marries Fezon, daughter of Duke Savary of Aquitaine.

Peter Breughel's painting *The Battle of Carnival and Lent* (1559) shows the story of Orson and Valentine being performed as a mummers' play in a village street. Orson is clad in vegetation as a Wild Man, and carries a club. The story was still well known in the nineteenth century, when a mural of Orson and Valentine was painted in Cardiff Castle. In Central Europe, the wild man appears in the *Wildmannspiel* ('Wild Man's Game') and *Wildmanntanz* ('Wild Man's Dance') in connection with driving out winter. At Kandersteg in Switzerland, for instance, the New Year guisers called *Pelzmarti* include a man called the Chrismaa. He is dressed from head to foot in branches of the Fir tree. Also bedecked with Fir branches are the masked Wild Men and Women called *Osemali* who appear during *Fasnacht* at Tannheim in the Schwarzwald of south Germany. Another kind of 'Green Man' appears in the midwinter in the Perchtenlauf of Pongau in Austria, where men called *Verchmanndl*, with blackened faces and dressed from head to foot in green lichens, climb on house roofs and push snow down upon unsuspecting bystanders.

There is actually a tenuous connection between Wild Men and the Ogham script itself. According to *Triocha-céad Corca Dhuibhne*, wild men were plentiful in the Barony of Corco Duibne in County Kerry in the west of Ireland, the place where ancient Ogham inscriptions are most plentiful. The archetypal Celtic wizard, Merlin, is also part of this complex motif of humans-in-trees. In the Welsh poem *Afallennau* (1250), we are told how, having lost his wits from witnessing the slaughter of battle, Merlin enters the Wood of Caledon. There, he becomes a wild man who hides in an Apple tree when he is hunted by King Rhydderch. Salaiin ar Foll, the divine madman of Le Folgoët in Brittany, a devotee of Our Lady who died in 1358, used to sit up in a tree above a holy well, praying.

The motif of the human face in the tree was adopted in Restoration England for the inn, tavern, alehouse and public house sign, *The Royal Oak*. This symbol arose in 1651, when, following his defeat in battle at Worcester, King Charles II fled and was hunted by Parliamentary soldiers. He escaped detection by hiding amid the branches of the great Oak tree at Boscobel in Worcestershire. After the restoration, the tree was revered by royalists as 'The Royal Oak', saviour of the British monarch.

The actual tree died in 1704 as the result of continuous depredations by relic-hunters. A descendent of the Royal Oak grows at Boscobel to-day. *The Royal Oak* remains as a popular name for inns throughout England, where the king's head is portrayed amid the foliage. The festival called *Royal Oak Day*, or *Oak Apple Day*, May 29th, commemorates the restoration

23, The Royal Oak, showing the face of King Charles II in the Boscobel Oak, is a favourite English inn and public house sign.

of King Charles II to the throne in 1660. It is customary to wear Oak leaves on that day, and a festival is held at Great Wishford in Wiltshire. There, it is celebrated with a procession and dancing, followed by ceremonial Oak branch-cutting.

In his monumental list (1864), the authority on English inn signs, Jacob Larwood, numbers 24 inns, taverns and public houses called Green Man in London alone. Writing in 1866, Larwood suggested that the *Green Man* sign was "perhaps originally *Jack-in-the-Green*; in other instances *Archer* or *Robin Hood*". He thought that the sign, *Wild Man* may have also been derived from these two. "For the sign of the *Green Man* there is a twofold explanation", wrote Larwood, "The first is that it represents the green, wild, or wood men of the shows and pageants, such as described by Machyn in his Diary on Lord Mayor's Day, 1553, and in the account of the festivities when Queen Elizabeth was at Kenilworth Castle in 1575. Besides wielding sticks with crackers in pageants, these green men sometimes fought with each other, attacked castles and dragons, and were altogether a very popular character with the public ..... the second version of this sign is that it is intended for a forester, a verderer or ranger, and in that garb the *Green Man* is now almost invariably represented". Corroborating Larwood, as early as the seventeenth century, London trade tokens bore images of the 'Green Man' as a forester. Robin Hood, dressed in his outlaw's livery of Lincoln Green (or, occasionally Kendal Green), also appeared as the 'Green Man'.

Some believe the inn sign *The Green Man* to be derived from the heraldic arms of the Distillers' Company, which was founded as a Livery Company of the City of London in 1709 (and ranks 87th in precedence). The supporters of the arms are two 'Indians' (Native Americans), for which sign painters frequently substituted foresters or 'wild men'. Larwood notes that *The Green Man and Still* in White Cross Street, London,

24. In many ways, the wizard Merlin, the wild orphan Orson and King Charles II are aspects of the Woodwose, or Wild Man, here shown wrestling with a Unicorn, symbol of purity.

once had a sign showing a forester drinking 'drops of life' (*Aqua Vitae*).

Another theory comes from Brewer, in *The Dictionary of Phrase and Fable*, where he states that the inn sign *The Green Man and Still* refers to the distillation of spirits from green herbs, such as Peppermint Cordial. The 'Green Man' in this meaning is thus the 'Greengrocer of Herbs', and the still is the apparatus in which the liquor is distilled.

Many *Gasthäuser* (inns) in south Germany, northern Switzerland and Austria are also called after the Wild Man - *Zum Wilden Mann*. Until they were driven out of business by modern medicine, Central European herbalists, mountebanks and quacks travelled through the land accompanied by assistants dressed as 'Wild Men'. This was done both as a means of advertising and as authentication of their potions and lotions, powders and pills, some of which were made by distilling herbs. During the eighteenth century, the Bavarian authorities felt that these travelling medicine-men were a menace, and so guising as the 'Wild Man' was prohibited by law. Perhaps there was once a similar connection with medicinal cures and this guiser in Britain. In the nineteenth century, the *Green Man* public house in Edgware Road, London, possessed a medicinal spring in its cellars, from which 'eye lotion' was provided, free of charge, to customers.

Lady Raglan's 1939 article linked her 'Green Man' with the figure of English traditional performance known as Jack-in-the-Green. The custom of Jack-in-the-Green is practised on May Day each year, when a man is dressed from head to foot in fresh green leaves and then parades with the morris dancers and other guisers in procession through the streets. Historically, as a May Day practice in England, Jack-in-the-Green cannot be traced back earlier than the eighteenth century, when the chimney-sweeps, especially in London, paraded on their traditional holiday, (described by Roy Judge

25. The Straw Bear, paraded annually in January at Whittlesey in Cambridgeshire (with part of the traditional tune behind).

in his influential study, *The Jack-in-the-Green* (1979)). A painting by John Collett, titled May Morning, (circa 1760) shows a May Day parade in London. It does not show a Jack-in-the-Green, but Milkmaids carrying bright copper- and silverware on their heads. Of course, Jack's absence here is not evidence of absence on that day elsewhere in London or anywhere else. A later London May Day painting, *Upper Lisson Street* (between 1837 and 1847) shows a fully-leafed Jack-in-the-Green with a floral crown on the apex of his costume, accompanied by a drummer, a blackened-faced boy, a ribbon-bedecked man and a Harlequin-like character with a mask. The relationship of Jack-in-the-Green with his 'Wild Men' counterparts in English and Continental pageants is still to be fully investigated.

As leaf-bedecked people walk or dance through the streets of village, town and city, their leaves are shed, symbolically spreading their new greenery. As a springtime manifestation of fertility, this parallels the grains and straw dropped by the Straw Bears of Whittlesey in England, Walldürrn, Wilflingen and elsewhere in Germany as they drive out winter and herald the coming growing season. Jacks-in-the-Green appear to-day in a major May festival at Hastings in Sussex, the Rochester Sweeps' Festival in Kent, in Oxford for the May Morning celebrations, and in many other places. A contemporary song in English traditional style, *Jack-in-the-Green*, written by Martin Graebe, is often performed along with the guising. At present, the 'Green Man' is a potent image in contemporary Paganism, where it represents a god of vegetation. The master mask-maker Justin Capp makes 'Green Man' masks which are used in rites and ceremonies.

# Chapter 5
# Celtic Tree-Lore of Birch, Thorn and Oak

## Birches of May and Summer

Although the custom remains most vigorous to-day in mainland Europe, May-Trees and their allies were set up in former times all over the Brythonic lands. As the primary tree, the Birch was favoured. A whole tree was cut down on May Eve. Then it was transported to the nearest village or town and set up. Its presence there on May Day was deemed necessary if fertility and prosperity were to crown the coming season. For a short time, the May-Tree recreates the forest within the town, bringing back to it the wild spirit of growth.

Traditions of Celtic festive trees are best recorded from Wales and along the Welsh borderlands in England. One of the earliest references we have is a fourteenth-century cywydd from the Bard Grufydd ap Adda ap Dafydd (died c. 1344), who laments the fate of a Birch that has been cut down to be the may-tree at Llanidloes. He contrasts its proper place, growing in the wood, with its new temporary location by the town's pillory.

In south Wales, the ceremony of setting up the May-Tree is called *Codi'r Fedwen*, 'raising the birch'. In north Wales, it is *Y Gangen Haf*, 'the summer branch'. It is traditional to bedeck *Y Gangen Haf* with the most precious possessions of the village, such as pocket watches, brooches, silver tankards and dishes. In the eighteenth century, William Robert o'r Ydwal, 'The Blind Poet of Llancarfan', described the raising of the Birch in his poem *Taplas Gwainfo*. The pole was trimmed by a carpenter until it was round, and then it was decorated with pictures. Young women then adorned it with ribbons and wreaths. A weather-cock with ribbons streaming from its tail was set on its apex, beneath which a banner was unfurled. Morris dancing, *dawns y fedwen* ('The Dance of the Birch') was performed beneath such May-Trees. Before the Great War put an end to the custom, Herefordshire farmers felled a tall thin Birch on May Day. They bedecked it with ribbons and set it up against the stable door to bring good luck for that year.

In addition to setting up Birchen Maypoles, Welsh custom also erects *Y fedwen haf*, the 'Summer Birch'. This is set up on the feast of St John at Midsummer (June 24th). European tradition does not restrict pole-erection to May or Midsummer. In Wales, three poles, painted red, white and green, are set up next to the road at the entrances of a village where an *Eisteddfod* is being held. At Fasnacht (Shrovetide) in south Germany, villages erect the *Narrenbaum* (Fools' Tree), identical with Maypoles except that they are bedecked with rags, and sometimes comic objects like chamber pots. They are cut down ceremonially on Shrove Tuesday. Other trees or poles are erected at Easter, Whitsun and Harvest, and the Christmas Tree, first brought into Britain from Germany and popularized in 1841 by Queen Victoria's husband, Prince Albert, is universal.

Although it has largely lapsed, there is an identical custom of the Midsummer Pole in Cornwall. A description of the tradition formerly kept up until 1725 in the Caple Hendre district of Llandybïe in Carmarthenshire tells of the scale of the Midsummer revels around the Birch. "The dance was to begin on St John's Day and to continue, if the weather were favourable, for nine days. There were one or two harpists, and the assembly, both male and female, used to dance. They used to set a birch tree in the earth and decorate its branches with wreaths of flowers".

In medieval Wales, lovers' bowers were made beneath Birch trees, and wreaths of Birch were given as tokens of love. "Before there was the law of a Pope or his trouble", *The Red Book of Hergest* tells us,

> "Each one made love,
> Without blame to his loved one.
> Free and easy enjoyment will be without blame,
> Well has May made houses of the leaves -
> There will be two assignations,
> Beneath trees of concealment,
> For me, myself and my dear one."

All over Europe, it is customary for the men of neighbouring parishes to attempt to cut down or steal their neighbours' May-Pole. If they succeed, then they have brought shame on the village whose pole is lost. Writing in 1842, Morgan Rhys noted, "it was considered a great disgrace for ages to the parish that lost its Birch, whilst, on the other hand, the parish that succeeded in stealing a decked bough, and preserving its own, was held up in great esteem ..... no parish that had once lost its Birch could ever hoist another, until it had succeeded in stealing one that belonged to some of the neighbouring parishes" (*The Cambrian Journal*, March, 1853). Such Maypole destruction continues in Germany today, when the local youths are not sufficiently vigilant against those of neighbouring villages for three nights after the pole is set up.

In Wales, the custom was accompanied by considerable violence. The diary of William Thomas (1727-1795), who lived at Michaelston-super-Ely, near St Fagans in the Cardiff region, tells of the attempted theft of the Summer Birch in

June 1768. The villagers of St Fagans were compelled to use firearms to protect their Birch against a mob of fifty men from nearby St Nicholas. A day or two later, the St Nicholas men were joined by others from Llancarfan and Penmark, so the defenders called in reinforcements from Llandaff and Cardiff.

## Besoms

Throughout Europe, besoms are far more than just utilitarian brooms for sweeping the floor. They are both revered and feared, having a part in many customs and traditions. In the British Isles, the original besoms are believed to have been made from the Broom plant (the Ogham 'On'). The traditional English Besom is made from three woods. The actual broomstick or *stale* is made of Ash, to which an array of Birch twigs are tied with Osiers (Willow). Thus, in Ogham terms, the Besom is made from Nin, Beith and Saille, three *Feadha* of the first *Aicme*, and all Kiln or peasant Trees.

In former times in East Anglia, the broom-tiers or *Broom Squires* made the brush-end of brooms from Ling (Heather), bound to the broomstick by long pliant bonds of split Bramble. In Ireland, it was customary to use a Heather besom to sweep the threshing-floor, and in Scotland, a Heather broom, called the *Broom-Cow*, is used in the game of Curling, for sweeping the ice in front of the moving stones. Occasionally, the twigs which compose the besom proper are made of Hazel (Coll) or Rowan (Luis), but Birch (Beith) is the best.

Generally, the besom has the apotropaic function of keeping out unwanted people or harmful supernatural beings. A Romani tradition recorded in Hampshire asserted that if an 'ill wisher' approached one's dwelling, then a besom laid across the threshold would prevent entry. Irish custom asserts that for protection against all mishaps, a broom should be leant against the dairy door whilst the milk is being churned. According to French folk-wisdom, because the besom sweeps away bad things, gradually it accumulates dirt and harmful powers, and becomes bad in itself. It then has the possibility to be used for evil purposes by malevolent individuals. Therefore, like most Maypoles, a fresh broom should be made each year.

Times of year for making new brooms vary from place to place. They vary from Twelfth Night (Westphalia and Mecklenburg, Germany); springtime in Switzerland; Old Bohemia (Czech Republic), Easter; in Austria, St George's Day (April 23rd); Rome, on Midsummer Day (St John's Day, June 24th). In England, it is considered inauspicious to make a new broom of Birch twigs or green Broom during the Twelve Days of Christmas or in the merry month of May. It is unlucky to sweep the house at all in May, for it will bring death: "If you sweep the house with broom in May, You'll sweep the head of the house away".

In German-speaking countries, besoms are not be left outside on Walpurgis Night (May Eve), because they might be used by witches who roam abroad on that night.

Just as the time of making new brooms is significant, so certain dates are considered important in sweeping-lore. Traditions of sweeping at New Year persist in northern England. At Laneshaw Bridge, near Colne in Lancashire, it is customary to sweep the old year out and the new year in. In former times, men, women and children went round from house to house on New Year's Eve between ten o'clock and midnight. Disguised with masks or blackened faces, the sweepers had the right to enter any house whose door was not fastened. If they encountered a locked door, they made a 'mumming' sound to encourage those inside to open up. Without a word or a song, the sweepers entered the part of the house where the family was, and dusted the room and the hearth. When they finished, they rattled their money-boxes and received largesse. In Handsworth, Sheffield, a mummer personating 'Little Devil Doubt', carrying a besom, sweeps out the houses.

"In comes I, Little Devil Doubt,
If you don't give me money,
I'll sweep you all out.
Money I want, and money I crave.
If you don't give me money,
I'll sweep you all to your grave!",

proclaims the besom-wielding Little Devil Doubt in *The Old Tup* mummers' play (version from Ecclesfield, Sheffield, 1893).

It is said in Eyam, Derbyshire that unless one sweeps the doorstep on the first of March, then the house will be infested with fleas for the rest of the year.

Sweeping magically with the besom is similar to sweeping dirt, except that luck is being swept rather than physical dust and detritus. Fastnacht *Narrenzünfte* (Fools' Guilds) in many places in south Germany include 'witches' with besoms who sweep away bad things, evil and winter. Traditional witchcraft in western England uses a besom or broom bundle made of Broom to sweep the circumference of 'magic circles' in which rituals are conducted. The besom has long been the emblem of the witch. In Ireland in 1323, Alice Kyteler of Kilkenny, was brought before a court accused of being a witch. An allegation made against was that she "swept the streets of Kilkenny between Compline and Twilight, raking all the filth towards the door of her son, William Outlawe, chanting, "to the house of William my son, hie all the wealth of Kilkenny Town"". By so doing, it was thought, she could accumulate others' riches magically in her son's house. Custom in the British Isles demands that dust should always be swept inwards across the threshold. If the sweeper should sweep the dust outwards, then she will sweep away the luck of the house. When the out-sweeper is a bride sweeping the house for the very first time, then disaster will follow.

In England and Wales, a besom is used to solemnize the customary common-law wedding. A Birch-twig besom must be propped up across an open doorway, either the bride's home, or another place in which the couple intend to live together. The man leaps over the broom into the house, followed by his bride. When they jump, they must touch neither the doorpost nor the broom. If this should happen, then the ceremony is invalid. 'Jumping the broomstick' must be performed in the presence of witnesses who ensure that the proper form is observed, and no touching takes place. Traditionally, formal separation can take place within twelve months of 'jumping the broomstick' by reversing the ceremony, and jumping out of the house over the besom, again in the presence of witnesses. The British Romani tradition also employs besoms in marriage ceremonies. Romani use a besom made from flowering Broom, which they lay on the ground. The couple, holding hands, jump backwards over it. An alternative rite sees the father of the bride holding a besom, which the couple, man first, leap over.

According to English traditional usage, a woman who wants to tell others that she is away from home places her broomstick against the door, with its twigs upwards, or, more rarely, protruding from the chimney. But this sign is said to give the husband or partner the freedom to associate with other women whilst the broom is up. Thus the expression "to hang out the besom" means for a man to have a sexual relationship with another woman whilst his wife is absent. Similarly, in France, the expression "rotir le balai" (to burn the besom) means to live a sexually promiscuous life. The English traditional songs, *Green Brooms* and *The Besom-Maker*, suggest that the trade of broom-cutting has erotic undertones.

The history of sexual arousal through Birching is poorly documented. The earliest publications on the subject in English appear to be *The Birchen Bouquet* (1780) and *Venus, Strict Mistress of Birchen Sports* (1788). In his *English Eroticism* (1984), Piero Lorenzoni estimates that around one hundred books about sexual Birching were published in England in the nineteenth century. These included *Colonel Spanker's Experimental Discourse* (1836), which tells of the exploits of the 'Society of Aristocratic Flagellants' in London's Mayfair, and Margaret Anson's book on an exclusively female secret society called *The Merry Order of St Bridget* (1857), whose initiations and ceremonies involved Birching.

Thus, the Birch is a symbol of sexuality, fertility and growth. It is said that children must never be chastised with besoms, or they will not grow. It was once believed that if an unmarried woman stepped across a besom on the ground, she would become an unmarried mother. At times of 'misrule', it was not uncommon in the past for naughty boys to place brooms at strategic places in the house where girls would cross them unknowingly. In Yorkshire to this day, calling a woman a 'besom' is an insult, meaning that she has borne a child out of wedlock, the result of a 'greenwood marriage', and in southern Scotland, a prostitute is called a "besom".

According to the Welsh Bardic tradition, the besom is symbolic of the twigs and branches of the Bardic alphabet, where it is called *Y Ddasgubell Rodd*. This is 'The Gift Besom' that symbolizes the sweeping-away of everything that conceals the truth. A Bardic text of uncertain date, published in 1866, gives a teaching concerning the *Ddasgubell Rodd* as a key to the 'Primitive Coelbren'. Here, as in its physical aspect, the besom is a symbol of transition, the creator of change.

## Fairy Thorns, Gentle Trees and Our Lady's Roses

Celtic lore tells of trees and bushes whose unusual outward form expresses an inner spiritual quality. Irish vernacular tradition recognizes that any lone Thorn tree growing in the middle of a stony field, or on a hillside, is the property of the fairies. Such trees are deemed especially venerable when they are growing by a large boulder or over a holy well. Also, Thorn trees that grow upon a hedge- or field-bank, denote a fairy place. When three or more Thorn trees grow together naturally to form an L- or V-shape, then they have done so under otherworldly influence. It is believed that otherworldly beings are present in certain trees. According to Cornish lore, people who buried treasure always planted a Hawthorn over it. This prevented the *Piskies* from taking it away. In Ireland, the sprites called *Lunantishees* guard the Blackthorn (Straif) bushes from unwarranted interference.

The holy Thorn trees known as 'Gentle Bushes', play an important part in vernacular religion. They are protectors of the locality, bringing the best possible fortune. Thorns play an important role in local lore. The Irish Bard Raftery sang the praises of the Killeaden Fairy Thorn of Lis Ard, and St Senan lay down to die under a Thorn-tree at Kil-eochaille near Rossbay, County Clare. As he was dying, he said "Let me lie here till dawn", and so his body was allowed to rest beneath the Thorn until the sun rose again.

Fairy Thorns should never be cut or damaged, even the fallen leaves and branches lying beneath them should not be taken away. Sometimes, a branch broken off accidentally will be tied back into its original position, rather than being removed. "Don't tamper with the lone bush", we are warned, for it is considered extremely unlucky to destroy a sacred tree. In former times, deep respect for these trees was a universal *geis*. If, for some reason, deliberate or accidental, the *geis* was broken, then appalling misfortune would befall the *geis-*

breaker. In addition to this, people, animals, plants and property in the locality of the tree would suffer. To fell a fairy tree is to risk releasing harmful forces that it holds in check. The resulting imbalance can take the form of poor crops, sickness in humans and animals and general misfortune. Only by planting a new tree of the same species at that place, using the proper rites and ceremonies, may the imbalance be rectified.

The lone Thorn tree that grows on Wearyall Hill at Glastonbury, visible for miles around, is a typical 'fairy tree'. The current Thorn is the descendent of a miraculous tree that legendarily had been planted by the first Christian in Britain, Joseph of Arimathea. The 'original' Thorn had two stems. In the early seventeenth century, one was cut down by a religious fanatic, who was punished immediately for his sacrilege. "He was well serv'd for his blind zeal", wrote James Howell in *Dodona's Grove* (1644), "who, going to cut down an ancient white *Hawthorn-tree*, which, because she *budded* before others, might be an occasion for *superstition*, had some of the *prickles* flew into his eye, and made him monocular". The rest of the Thorn was cut down by Cromwell's followers. But by then, devout people had taken the precaution of growing new bushes from cuttings, and a descendent still grows in the churchyard of St John's in Glastonbury High Street. Like its forebears, it blossoms around midwinter, and cuttings are sent to the reigning monarch. Others grow in various parts of England, and blossom at the same time.

Dermot Mac Manus recounts in his book,*The Middle Kingdom* (1958), the story of the Thorn tree that was cut down to clear the ground for a new hospital at Kiltimagh. Although he was warned not to do it, the workman felled the Thorn, only to suffer a stroke which led to his death. The place at which this occurred was considered to be cursed by the sacrilege, and the building erected there never served as a hospital. Many years later, in the early 1970s in Ulster, a fairy Thorn was cut down

26. The four faces of the ninth-century Celtic cross at Nevern Pembrokeshire, with interlace and key-patterns that reflect 'the wattles and the branches' of British Bardic tradition.

because the 'greenfield site' was required to build a new car factory. It was the place of manufacture of the ill-fated DeLorean car, which cost the taxpayer dear when it went out of business shortly after production commenced.

That trees can be the receptacle of spirit is demonstrated by the holy well of St Fintan at Clonemagh in County Laois, Ireland. This, 'holy well' was half-way up a tree. Of course, according to literalist perceptions, a tree cannot contain a well, for no water can flow from it. But St Fintan's well-tree came into being when the holy well nearby was profaned and ceased to flow. Water appeared in a crook of the tree into which the spirit of St Fintan migrated, and it was recognized with rites and ceremonies appropriate to a holy well.

Two of the major pardons of East Morbihan in Brittany celebrate miraculous religious images connected with trees. The Pardon of Notre-Dame-de-la-Tronchaye at Rochefort-en-Terre commemorates a black madonna discovered in a hollow tree during the twelfth century. At Josselin, the Pardon of Notre-Dame-du-Roncier, reveres 'Our Lady of the Bush'. The legend of Josselin tells how, by accident, a ploughman discovered an image of Our Lady in a Rose bush. He took the image home, but during the night, like an *Alraun*, it transported itself back again to the bush. After several fruitless journies, it was decided to make a shrine at the rose-bush. It soon gained a reputation for curing people from epilepsy. The Revolutionaries burned the image in 1793, but a fragment was retrieved from the ashes by a devotee, and this is enshrined to-day in a modern chapel on the site of the Rose bush. *Dris*, the Hedge- or Dog-Rose is one of the 'bushes' recognized by the Brehon Law of Ireland.

Another miraculous Rose bush was the origin of the veneration of Our Lady at the pilgrimage shrine of Ave Maria at Deggingen, south Germany. In the fourteenth century, a thorn-bearing Rose bush of ancient veneration was about to

27. The Water of Life, guarded by Sirona, Celtic goddess of holy wells that contain the healing power of Grannos Apollo, the Sun.

be cut down. But when the woodsman noticed the words 'Ave Maria' on each leaf, this was recognized as a divine sign. Instead of cutting down the Rose, it was venerated. Later, a chapel, now called Alt-Ave was erected by Franciscan monks at the site. A Rose bush grew by the north wall of Alt-Ave until 1996, when the area around the chapel was cleared during renovation work, and it was destroyed. The image of the miraculous plant, formerly painted on the chapel's altar, was covered over with grey paint at the same time.

## Dancing Trees and Trained Trees

English folk-tradition tells that several ancient buildings were built on living trees. They include the Old Manor House at Knaresborough in Yorkshire, the hall of Huntingfield in Suffolk and the Cross Keys Inn at Saffron Walden in Essex. In western England, especially near the Devon-Cornwall border, it was the custom to alter certain trees as they grew. In his *A Book of Devon* (1909), S. Baring-Gould described one of them, the Cross Tree at Moreton Hampstead: "The tree is an Elm, and it grows out of the basement of the old village cross, the lower steps of which engirdle the trunk ... the Elm, grown to a considerable size, was pollarded and had its branches curiously trained, so that the upper portion was given the shape of a table. On this tree-top it was customary on certain occasions to lay a platform, railed round, access to which was obtained by a ladder, and on this tree-top dancing took place". Baring-Gould quotes entries from a local journal that tell how the 'Dancing Tree' was used: "August 28th, 1801. - The Cross Tree floored and seated round, with a platform, railed on each side, from the top of an adjoining garden wall to the tree, and a flight of steps in the garden for the company to ascend. After passing the platform they enter under a grand arch formed of boughs. There is sufficient room for thirty persons to sit around, and six couples to dance, besides the orchestra. From the novelty of this rural apartment it is expected much company will resort there during the summer." Sadly, the

Moreton Hampstead Cross Tree was destroyed in a gale on October 1, 1891.

Other places in Devon also had 'dancing trees'. "On the high road from Exeter to Okehampton", wrote Baring-Gould, "near Dunsford, is a similar tree, but an Oak, and this was woven and extended and fashioned into a flat surface". According to local lore, the Fulford family of Great Fulford, held their lands on condition that they should dine once a year on top of this Oak, and hold a dance there for their tenants. Another such tree, 'The Meavy Oak', grew near to the village of Lifton on the road from Okehampton to Launceston. Said to be the earliest tree to put forth leaves in springtime, it was next to an inn called *The Royal Oak*. During festivities, the Meavy Oak, otherwise the Gospel Oak, supported a platform augmented by pillars. There was yet another similar Oak at Trebursaye, near Launceston, in Cornwall. It was said to be haunted by the ghost of a woman who had fallen from it during a dance, and perished.

Holy trees were important places of worship in the elder faith, and the traditions were continued in modified form in the Christian church. Gospel Oaks are places where religious services are or were held at certain times of year. Until the nineteenth century, marriages were conducted beneath an Oak at Brampton in Cumbria. Earlier Maytide customs all over Merry England saw many a 'greenwood marriage' (or 'Mad-Merry Marriage') conducted at such trees without Christian clergy being present. A service is held annually at Old Polstead Gospel Oak in Suffolk, and the practice continues in many other places, particularly in south Germany, where outdoor services are conducted at notable Oaks on Whitsunday.

In mainland Europe, trees, especially Lindens (Lime Trees, *Tilia platyphyllos*), were altered to take the form of a series of circular platforms, one above the other. Their shape reproduced the traditional 'cosmic axis', where the different planes of spiritual existence are 'stacked' one on top of the other (as taught in Bardic tradition). Such trees are recorded as far back as the year 1200, where, in his Arthurian epic *Parzival*, Wolfram von Eschenbach gives the account of how Sigune sits weeping in the crown of a Linden with the corpse of her lover. Dating from around 1501 in Queen Anne of Brittany's *Book of Hours* is an illuminated page by Jean Bourdichon that shows a Maying scene. Two youths are coming out of woodland carry flowering 'May Branches'. Nearby grows a three-tiered tree, on which hang suspended eggs and apples. Speed's map of the town of Flint, in north Wales (1610), shows one, along with a maypole and stocks in the central square outside the church. Living examples have survived into modern times in the Netherlands and parts of Germany, and although most have disappeared, there are a number of new ones growing to-day.

# Chapter 6
# Welsh Bardic Scripts

*"The three things which a Bard ought to make with his own hands are the Coelbren, the roll and the Plagawd".*
Bardic Triad.

### A Brief Overview of Bardic Scripts
The entire body of ancient Celtic lore and legend was transmitted from mouth to ear, without being written down. The oldest written texts contain material that may have existed in oral form for centuries, perhaps millennia, before being committed to writing. Most ancient written sources contain legends, history, genealogies and tales of the gods. From written sources alone, it is reasonable to assert that Bardo-Druidic tradition has a continuity from at least the sixth century CE.

The secret initiated traditions, jealously guarded, were not consigned to writing until much later, if at all. Also, the vagaries of history have meant that what comes down to us from ancient times must, of necessity, be but a fragment of what has existed over time. It is clear that many, if not most, texts have come into being and passed away without trace. Only when copies have been made, have texts survived, and then sometimes, only fragmentarily. In addition, transcribers and collators often added material where it was lacking, or corrected what they believed to be wrong. In this area, Bardic inspiration has a quite different approach than academic scholarship, and it is wrong to judge it according to the latter's criteria.

The eighteenth century stonemason, Edward Williams, who wrote under his Bardic name, Iolo Morganwg, according to the "privilege and usage of the Bards of the Isle of Britain", is a good example of this. He is a key figure in the history of both the Welsh *Eisteddfod*, which he re-established in London in 1792, and in the development of Celtic spirituality, including contemporary Druidry. Over many years, Iolo collected together, compiled, edited, and added to texts which he had received both orally and in manuscript from other preservers of Welsh culture. It was with this knowledge that he re-stated or developed the Bardic knowledge that underlies contemporary Druidic teachings.

At the end of the eighteenth century, Iolo was one of the two members of the *Bardic Institution*, the other being the Reverend Edward Evan of Aberdare. The *Eisteddfod* organized by Iolo in 1792, which is the direct forerunner of the contemporary Welsh *Eisteddfodau*, was convened on Primrose Hill near London (now part of Regent's Park) at *Alban Elfed*, the autumnal equinox. It brought together Welsh and English Bards and Druids in a bilingual (Welsh and English) celebration of British Bardism. A few years later, Welsh Druids declared that only Welsh was the proper language of Bardism, and the English Bards and Druids were barred from further participation. The concept that "the Red Dragon has two tongues" had not yet emerged. There was thus a split in the Bardic current that Iolo had brought together. Both the Welsh Druids and the English Druids proceeded on their own pathways, which they continue to do to-day, for, as the Druid Colin Murray remarked to me in 1978, "England is also a Celtic country".

*The* promoters of the Welsh National Eisteddfod at Llangollen in 1858, offered a prize of £30 and a Bardic tiara in gold for

28. The Tablets of the Bards, with Llawdden's 37-character Coelbrei Y Beirdd.

the "fullest illustration from original sources of the theology, discipline and usages of the Bardo-Druidic system in the Isle of Britain". Only one text was received, from an unknown Bard called Plennydd. The Bardic judges of the Eisteddfod, chaired by Myvyr Morganwg, deemed the text authentic: "The compiler has been very diligent, and remarkably successful in obtaining access to such a vast number of ancient manuscripts bearing on Bardism....with respect to the genuineness, Plenydd justly observes, "though their authors cannot in many instances be named, any more than we can name the authors of the Common Law of England, yet the existence of the peculiar dogmas and usages which they represent may be proved from the compositions of the Bards from the era of Taliesin down to the present time."

It emerged subsequently that the text was the work of none other than the late Iolo Morganwg (the so-called *Iolo Manuscripts*). His great work was published at Llandovery in 1866 under the title, *Barddas, or, a Collection of Original Documents, Illustrative of the Theology, Wisdom and Usages of The Bardo-Druidic System of the Isle of Britain*. Later academics who examined *Barddas* claimed that they could not find any of Iolo's sources, and thus, his work must be a forgery (in their understanding of textual authenticity). However, the Bardic judges of 1858 had already taken this into account, and dismissed the possibility. But, whatever their origin, the teachings in *Barddas* exist in their own right. Morganwgian Druidry has existed now for over two centuries, and has always been the significant element in the British Druidic movement.

According to Morganwgian Bardic tradition, the principal collator of ancient Welsh writings was the sixteenth century Bard, Llewellyn Sion of Llangewydd. When he was young, Llewellyn Sion was a student of the Bards Thomas Llewelyn of Rhegoes and of Meurig Davydd of Llanisan. Both of these men were eminent Bards of the Glamorgan Chair. Llewellyn

Sion was a worthy successor, gaining recognition as a composer of elegant verse. His fame as a Bard gained him employment making and selling transcripts of collectable Welsh manuscripts. His work brought him into contact with eminent collectors of ancient Welsh manuscripts, to which he was given free access. Llewellyn Sion was thus enabled to make copies, so preserving many texts that otherwise might have been destroyed. For instance, Sir William Herbert invited Llewellyn Sion to Rhaglan Castle to study his major collection of manuscripts. Later, it was completely destroyed by fire during Cromwell's civil war.

In 1560, Llewellyn Sion took over the honour of presiding in the the Bardic Chair of Glamorgan. He wrote a book which collated together much of the information that he had gleaned from the ancient texts. Titled *Atgofion Gwybodau yr Hen Gymry*, by all accounts it was a major treatise on ancient Welsh traditional knowledge. It dealt with classical Welsh poetry, genealogy, memorials, agriculture, customary law, medicine, chemistry and handicrafts. Unfortunately, it was never published. It seems that the manuscript was sent to London for publication. But during preparation, Llewellyn Sion died at an advanced age, and the book never appeared. However, parts of the work survived in some form or another until the eighteenth century, when they were collated by Welsh Bardic scholars, including Iolo. It is from them that we have our present knowledge of the *Coelbren Y Beirdd*, the Welsh Bardic 'alphabets'. Unlike Ogham and the Runes, however, *Coelbren* works at a deeper symbolic level, and does not attempt to be an inventory of reality.

## Divine Origins

According to the tradition, the characters of the *Coelbren Y Beirdd* are derived from the basic structure of existence, brought into the world of humans through mystic revelation. Bardo-Druidic teachings state that the origin of letters was simultaneous with the creation of the universe. They are a manifestation of a primal vibration, which, according to Celtic Christian mysticism, is the Word of God. This tradition is explained in *Barddas*, as follows:

*"When God pronounced his name, with the word sprang the light and the life, for previously, there was no life but God himself. And the way it was spoken was of God's direction. His name was pronounced, and with the utterance was the springing of light and vitality, and man, and every other living thing; that is to say, each and all sprang together."*

From the light, which Bardo-Druidry deems the most perfect manifestation of the divine, came the revelation of the concept of writing:

*"Menw Hen ap y Menwyd (Menw the Aged, son of Menwyd), beheld the springing of the light, and its form and appearance.... in three columns; and in the rays of light, the vocalization - for one were the hearing and seeing, one in unison with the form and sound was life, and one unitedly with these three was power, which power was God the Father. And by seeing the form, and in it hearing the voice - not otherwise - he knew what form and appearance voice should have...And it was on hearing the sound of the voice, which had in it the kind and utterance of three notes, that he obtained the three letters, and knew the sign that was suitable to one and other of them. Thus he made in form and sign the Name of God, after the semblance of rays of light, and perceived that they were the figure and form and sign of life.....It was from the understanding thus obtained in respect of this voice, that he was able to assimilate mutually every other voice as to kind, quality and reason, and could make a letter suitable to the utterance of every sound and voice. Thus were obtained the Cymraeg* (Welsh), *and every other language."*

This Bardo-Druidic 'creation myth' differs from other European myths of the same kind, in that it does not describe the making of matter by a physical Demiurge or Creator, but the springing of human awareness of it. To the Bards, 'creation' is the 'springing of the light', the moment when the human witness who beholds the divine act gains conscious awareness of existence. Creation is the arrival of consciousness, that moment at which everything that exists could now be seen and described. This sacred story recognizes the interrelatedness and essential oneness of all things in existence, as defined by consciousness. The definition of existence by 'the utterance of every sound and voice' was the foundation of transmittable human culture, the beginning of history, for word and symbol enable the past to be recalled, the present to be defined, and transmitted into times yet to come.

The Holy Name of God, from which all things were held to emanate, was rarely spoken by monotheistic Druids or Celtic Christians out of respect and for fear of the consequences of taking a holy name 'in vain':

*"It is considered presumptuous to utter this name in the hearing of any man in the world. Nevertheless, every thing calls him inwardly by this name - the sea and land, earth and air, and all the visibles and invisibles of the world, whether on the earth or in the sky - all the worlds of all of the celestials and the terrestrials - every intellectual being and existence..."*

The Welsh name of God was symbolized by the *Awen*. This is the primary Bardic and Druidic sigil, written as three lines radiating from above. Each of the three lines of the *Awen* have a specific meaning: "Thus are they made", Barddas recounts, " - the first of the signs is a small cutting or line inclining with the sun at eventide, thus \ ; the second is another cutting, in the form of a perpendicular, upright post, I; and the third is a cutting of the same amount of inclination as the first, but in an opposite direction, that is, against the sun, thus / and the three placed together, thus /|\ ." Together, the *Awen* represents conscious awareness, symbolically the threefold or triadic nature of existence. Past, present and future can only be recognized by conscious beings.

The *Awen* also has an alphabetic form - OIV. Its Bardo-Druidic explanation is that O was given in the first column of light, I to the second or middle light-column, and V to the third. "It was by means of this word that God declared his existence, life, knowledge, power, eternity and universality", *Barddas* recounts, "*And in the declaration was his love, that is coinstantaneously with it sprung like lightning all the universe into life and existence, co-vocally and co-jubilantly with the uttered Name of God, in one united song of exultation and joy - then all the worlds to the extremities of Annwn.*"

### Practical Developments

Although these letters were divine in origin, they were insufficient for writing useful texts. The invention of Welsh writing proper is attributed to Einigan Gawr (Einigan the Giant). Legend tells how Einigan invented writing to preserve the memory of the life of his father, Huon, son of Alser. He seems to have made the invention in mainland Europe, for Llewellyn Sion tells how: "He came to his father's kindred in the Isle of Britain, and exhibited his art, and they adjudged him to be the wisest of the wise and called him Einigan Wyddon (Einigan the Wise)". Einigan's record was made by carving letters into wood (the old word *pren*). Both the letters and the tabets on which they were written were called *Coelbren* 'the wood of credibility'.

Like the Ogham and Runic scripts, Coelbren is composed of angular letters designed to be cut easily in wood or stone. In Barddas, the section *Awgrym* (Symbol) tells us, "The best wood in respect to the facility of chipping and grooving is

29. Menw hen ap Menw witnessing the springing of the light symbolizing the vital instant when human beings gained conscious awarenes of existence.

Hazel wood....or Willow wood.....the best of all Willows is the Yellow Willow. The ancient Poets, however, sought the Mountain Ash [Rowan], regarding it as charmed wood, because worms will not devour or corrupt it, and because no vain spirit, or wicked fiend, will abide where there is Mountain Ash, and because neither charm nor enchantment can avail against Mountain Ash, nor injure it, nor him who carries it, because no deadly poison can touch them."

According to *Cyfrinach Y Beirdd - Lluniad Llythyrenau* (*The Bardic Secret - Formation of Letters*), the original letters were very simple, being derived from the three basic forms of the *Awen*. Bardic lore tells how the ancient Celts had only ten characters in their letter-row before they migrated to Britain. This story concurs with the legend of Einigan Gawr, who devised writing in mainland Europe. This continental Celtic alphabet may have been derived from Greek, which was used by certain Gallic Druids for inscriptions and calendars. It seems to have been a Bardic secret, for, even after the Coelbren was devised, these ten characters were revered as special. The earliest form of British *Coelbren* comprised sixteen characters, in the form of rays of light. Individual Bardic characters they called *Llythyrau*, from *lly*, meaning 'various' or 'apparent'; and *tyr*, 'to cut'. Another name for the letter-row is *Abcedilros*, from the letter-order. Later Bardo-Druidic interpretations saw these letters, derived from the *Awen*, as a synaesthetic experience: "Accordingly the memory of seeing could thus take place simultaneously with the memory of hearing; and, by means of signs, every sound of voice could be rendered visible to the eye..."

According to this legendary history,the sixteen-character Coelbren was devised during the reign of the British king Dyfnwal Moelmud ap Dyfnvarth ap Prydain ap Aeth Mawr. He is better known as the lawgiver Dunvallo Molmutius, who, according to Geoffrey of Monmouth's *Historia Regum Britanniae* (c.1136), reigned 430 - 390 BCE. Later, in the reign of Beli Mawr ap Manog (King Beli the Great, son of Manogan), the secret of this sixteen-character 'alphabet' was 'divulged' to non-initiates. Then, each letter was revised, and given a new, public, form. Because the secret was out, it was announced that forthwith there should be no king, judge or teacher in the country who could not read and understand the esoteric meanings of this alphabet.

Once the 'alphabet' was in general use, sixteen characters proved insufficient. Two further characters were added before the time of Taliesin (sixth century CE). At this period, with the introduction of the Christian religion, the cipher OIV came into use as the Name of God. According to one account, Taliesin enlarged the alphabet by adding a further two characters: "The language of twenty letters is in *Awen*", he wrote. However, the introduction of the twenty-character *Coelbren* is also ascribed to Ithel felyn (Ithel the Tawny). Bardo-Druidic lore teaches that this version of *Coelbren* continued in use until the knowledge and use of Latin as an everyday language ceased in Britain. It is notable that the earliest and most widespread version of Ogham also had twenty 'characters'.

Geraint fardd Glás (Geraint, the Blue Bard, who flourished around 900 CE), is credited with enlarging the character-set further by adding four 'auxiliary symbols'. These resemble the five For*feadha* of Ogham. This new *Coelbren* of twenty-four characters was used by Bards for 'black and white' (writing in ink) until the late middle ages. It was this version that the Bards employed for secret communication among themselves. It also appeared in the form of dice, used for divination. The Bardic tradition tells of the *Five Ages of Letters*. The first of these was the age of three letters, when the *Awen*, representing the godhead, was taken as the basis of writing. The second age of letters used sixteen characters. The third age began when two further letters were added, making eighteen, and the fourth age used twenty-four characters.

Finally, in the fifth age, the final development of *Coelbren* expanded it to thirty-eight characters. This was described by the Bard Ieuan Llawdden, Rector of Machynlleth, who flourished around 1440 to 1480. This long character set had a limited function, being used only for carving on wood. The twenty-four character row remained the standard form.

## The Bards' Wood in Language and Metaphor

The importance of wood-lore cannot be overstated in Celtic tradition. In Welsh, many words concerning consciousness, wisdom or learning in contain the element wydd, 'wood'. These include *arwydd*, a sign; *cyfarwydd*, skillful; *cyfarwyddyd*, information; cywydd, a revelation; *dedwydd*, having received knowledge; *derwydd*, a druid; *egwyddawr*, an alphabet; *gwyddon*, a wise man; and *gwynwyddigion*, men of sacred knowledge. Throughout recorded history, at least since the time of Taliesin, the Bards of the Island of Britain have used the metaphor of 'wood' to describe words, especially poetry. "I love the branches and the tight wattles", wrote Taliesin, meaning the characters of Bardic writing and the material on which they were made. The twelfth century Bard, Rhys Goch ab Riccert (1140 - 1170), wrote:

> "The wooden axe of an unpolished bard,
> Has been hewing a song to Gwenllian."
> Another famous bard, Iolo Goch (1315-1402), stated:
> "I will bear for Owain
> In metrical words, fresh and slow,
> Continually, not the hewing of Alder wood,
> By the chief carpenter of song."

Dafydd ab Gwilym (1340-1400) said, "This will address them on wood", whilst Rhys Goch Eryri (1330-1420) wrote: "No longer will be seen the mark of the axe of the flower of the carpenters on a song-loving and wise one", and Ieuan du'r

30. Bardo-Druidic cosmology is embedded within the structure of all Celtic artifacts, most explicitly in sacred structures such a cauldrons, shrines, croziers, healing-stones, reliquaries and crosses.

Bilwg (1460-1500): "May thy praise go - thou art a soldier - Upon wood, as long as day and water continue". In 1530, Harri ap Rhys Gwilym spoke of "The degrees and roll of wood-knowledge, The root of sciences, for the weaving of a song of praise"

## Alternative Forms: Pyrography, Stone and Plagawd

In addition to carving *Coelbren* characters onto wood, the Bards developed a system of pyrography using hot iron stamps. This technique may have been developed from coin dies or the stamps and moulds used in pottery. If it is as ancient as Bardic tradition makes it, then it may be the first example of 'movable type' printing in the world. Legendary history dates it from before the Roman occupation of Britain (43 - 410 CE): "It was in the time of Llyr Llediaith ('Llyr of Defective Speech) that the way of burning the *Cyrven* with an iron stamp was understood, that is, there was an iron for every letter, heated red hot, with which they burnt on an Ebill or a board what was required; and sometimes they formed letters on wood with the small prickings of a hot fork".

Although no indisputable ancient inscriptions exist in the Bardic *Abcedilros*, in cases where they written on slate, or carved in stone, they are called *Coelvain*, and the stones on which they are carved, *Peithynvain*, 'the stone of elucidation'. "They wrote with a steel pencil on both surfaces of the stones", *Awgrym* recounts, "and then put them on a strong cord, or on an iron or brass rod, which passed through the top of every *Peithynvain*. This infers that the 'stones' were flat slates. In the tenth century CE, Blegywryd, Archdeacon of Llandaff and King Hywel Dda's clerk, "faced the hall of the prince's court with stones, one side and another of the hall, and on the stones wrote in order, with a strong pencil, the laws which Hywel imposed upon the country and nation of the Cymry, an open entrance being left for every man that needed....whether a native or a stranger, to proceed into the hall, and to read the law, or to have it read to him". Hence it became customary to inscribe a vocal song, a Roll, a poem, the memorials of praiseworthy deeds, and the narration of wisdom, on *Peithynvain*, and to place them on the face of walls and partitions, or on strings, or iron rods".

King Arthur is said to have had the "system of the Round Table", and the praiseworthy deeds of its knights, written on plates of brass and tin. They were displayed in his three principal courts, at Caerleon-upon-Usk, Cellwig (Pendennis Castle) and Penrhyn Rhionydd (Glasgow). In former times at Caernarfon was the 'stone of enigmas', the tomb-slab of the ancient Welsh astronomer Gwydon ap Don. It was carved with letters only intelligible to the Bards.' Secret *Coelvains*' were also made in stone. They were comparable with the 'Charms of the Bards', small stones bearing Bardic characters, which were arranged appropriately to convey information. Sometimes, these messages were encrypted further to minimise the chances of unwelcome readers.

Although wood was always the medium of choice for Bardic poetry, other writing materials became available in Britain during the Roman occupation (44 - 410 CE). Bardic tradition tells how Bendigaidfran, father of the famed Celtic king Caradog (Caractacus), brought the technique of writing on parchment scrolls to Britain. Bendigaidfran learnt the technique during his seven years' captivity in Rome as a hostage on behalf of his son. On his return to Britain, he taught the indigenous scribes how to prepare goat skins for parchment. Although it was more convenient than wood, the more conservative Bards would not use the new technique. This refusal by the Bards to change their materials led to their writings being called *Coelbren y Beirdd*, literally, 'the wood-script of the Bards', as contrasted with Latin writings on parchment.

Bardo-Druidic history tells that paper was invented by a citizen of Constantinople called Moran. He devised a technique of grinding up flax and spreading it out thinly to make sheets of paper. Like parchment, flax paper was also used in Britain. But it was always considered inferior to another writing material, *Plagawd*: "*Plagawd* was a plant of the lily kind, which was brought over from India; and on it they wrote with black, or some other colour. After that, *Plagawd* of skin was made, being manufactured by art". According to some accounts, *Plagawd* originated in Egypt, not India, so it may have been Papyrus. Once *Plagawd* was imported, we are told, writing on trees was marginalized. Only the Bards maintained the tradition, out of an inner understanding that the medium is significant. In medieval times, only a few of them continued the tradition, and most Bards wrote in ink on parchment or paper.

## The Return of Wood-Wisdom

According to Llewellyn Sion, after the defeat in 1400 of the uprising led by the Welsh nobleman Owain Glyndwr (1349 - 1415), the Lancastrian king of England, Henry IV, forbade the importation of paper or *Plagawd* into Wales, and its manufacture there. He did this to prevent learning and written communication between Welsh people, or with foreigners. In addition, Bards were forbidden to travel around their normal circuits, or to make official visits to families, as in former times. However, this attempt to extirpate Welsh culture was counter-productive, for its consequence was the reinstatement of the use of the *Coelbren* of the Bards of the Isle of Britain. According to Welsh commentators, persecution of Welsh culture by the king of England actually encouraged the reinstatement of the ancient letters.

According to ninteenth century Welsh Bards, the construction of Coelbrens was seen as an act of cultural resistance against the English-speaking ruling class: "After recovering the knowledge of the Coelbrens, that is, the one of the Bards and the one of the Monks, nearly every person, male and female, wished to learn and construct them. From thence, they became the trade of sieve-makers and basket-makers, and upon them was cut the record of everything that required the preserved memorial of letter and book. And thus it was until the time of Henry the Seventh, who, being a Welshman, took his countrymen under the protection of his courtesy, and placed them, at his own expense, under the instruction of monks, and furnished them gratuitously with as much paper and parchment as was required; and they were taught whatever they would of the two languages, Welsh or English, and many learned both. On that account the knowledge of letters was more frequent among the common people of Wales than of England."

## Making and Using Bardic Frames

The making of Bardic Frames was described by Llewelyn Sion: "They gathered rods of Hazel or Rowan in the winter", he wrote, "about a cubit in length, and split each into four parts, that is, the wood was made into four splinters, and kept them, until by the working of time they became quite dry. Then they planed them square, in respect of breadth and thickness, and afterwards trimmed down the angles to the tenth part of an inch, which was done [in order] that the cuttings of the letters, that is, the symbols, which were cut with the knife on one of the four square surfaces, should not encroach visibly upon the next face; and thus on every one of the four faces. Then they cut the symbols, according to their character, whether they were those of language and speech, or of numbers, or other signs of art, such as the symbols of music, of voice and string. And after cutting ten such bars as were required, they prepared four splinters, two and two, which were called Pill, planed them smooth, placed two of them together side by side across the frame, and marked the places for ten holes. After that, they cut the holes, that is, half of each of the ten holes, in one splinter, and the same in the other; and they did the same with the other two splinters; and these are called *Pillwydd*. Then they took the symbolized or lettered bars, and made a neck at each of the two ends of every bar, all round, the breadth of a finger, along the bar.

Then they placed the lettered sticks by their necks on one of the *Pillwydd* at one end, and in like manner at the other end; and on that the other *Pillwydd* at each end, hole for hole. And on both ends of the two *Pillwydd*en they made necks, as places for strings to tie them firmly together at each end of the symbolized sticks. And when the whole are thus bound tight together, the book that is constructed in this manner is called *Peithynen*, because it is framed; the *Pillwydd* at each end keeping all together, and the *Ebillion*, or lettered staves [also known as *Peithwydd*, 'open' or 'elucidative wood' - NCP] turning freely in the *Pillwydd*, and thus being easy to read. That is, one face of the *Ebill* is read first, according to the number of its face, then it is turned with the Sun, and the second face is read, and it is turned so for every other face, and thus from *Ebill* to *Ebill* until the reading is finished. A number from one to ten being on the turning face of each of the *Ebillion*, the numbered face is the first that is to be read, and then the others in the order of their course with the Sun".

"The best wood wherewith to construct a *Peithenyn*, *Awgrym* tells us, "are young Oak saplings, as thick as would leave the *Ebillion* large enough, after the tree has been split into four parts, and the rind and epidermis completely chipped off from each quarter. They should be well dried before they are finished and lettered: the best time to cut the wood is the Feast of St Mary".

"There are forty sides to the *Ebillion* in every *Peithynen*", Llewelly Sion continues, "after that, another *Peithynen* is formed, until the conclusion of the poem or narrative. And where than more than ten *Ebillion* are required, and less

141

31. Peithenyn, the Bardic Frame.

than a score, as many *Ebillion* as are required are placed altogether in one entire *Peithenyn*. The reason for assigning ten as the particular number of succession, is, that ten is the division-point of number, and under the number of decades are all numbers arranged, until language cannot give them names."

## Other Secret Systems

Because *Coelbren* was divulged to the common people after being kept secret for centuries, in addition to the *Peithenyn*, the Bards developed other clandestine means of communication. Very small *Ebillion* were employed for intimate non-verbal communication by initiates. They were "a finger long", and had notches "so that they may be used by two persons or more, who are confidants. It is by placing and joining them together...that words and phrases are formed... they are called The Charms of the Bards, or Bardic Mystery". The Bards used these charms to create words for others to read. They also had a use in divination, a function that was facilitated by another variant, the *Coelbren of Simple Characters*.

The *Coelbren of Simple Characters* consists of individual pieces of wood, usually cubic in form, with single *Coelbren* characters on each face. A common version used a set of four cubic dice, with one face for each of the twenty-four characters: "Every one of the pieces was four sided, having six surfaces to each, and a letter on each surface, differently coloured, so that what was wanted might be obtained at first sight without much searching. The arrangement of twenty-four was found to be the best for those *Coelbrens*; and for obtaining mutual knowledge by means of the said *Coelbrens* secrets were ascertained, which caused much astonishment as to how it was possible." Another name for this is the *Palm Coelbren*, defined as "that where twenty-four are cut on small dice, that is inasmuch as each die has six sides, and a letter on each side, there will be on the four dice twenty-four letters, besides what may be obtained otherwise, when the die is reversed, in order to show a different letter.....by holding some of these in the palm of the hand, and putting them together in the presence of a man of secrecy, dumb conversation can be carried on."

## Postscript

It is not the intention of the writer to detail the methods of divination which may be applied to the Ogham and Coelbren systems. Ogham has been dealt with at length in both Liz and Colin Murray's *Celtic Tree Oracle* (Rider, 1988), and Nigel Jackson's and the present author's *The New Celtic Oracle* (Capall Bann, 1997). The use of the Welsh Bardic 'alphabets' as a divination system is more problematical because the individual letters are not specifically tied to a descriptive system like the trees of the Ogham. Divination with the Gaelic *Aibítir* is related closely to the Ogham methods.

Bardic tradition appears to have used the *Coelbrens* in the manner of the *Oracle of the Prenestine Fortune*, which was introduced to Europe by Egyptians and practised by the Etruscans at the oracle-centre of Preneste in Italy. This used cubes of Laurel wood, upon which were written letters. They were drawn at random from a bowl of silver, the metal sacred to Isis, the Egyptian goddess who presided over the oracle. Each letter was taken as the first letter of a word, and long oracular sentences were thereby constructed. Whether the *Coelbrens* actually originated in the oracle of Preneste is unknown. It is likely that, as a system of divination, the Runes did. If we believe in the philosophical idea of perfection, then we must recognize that all systems that attempt to arrange and describe the complexity of existence must fall short of this goal. However carefully it may be arranged, every description is flawed, because it is impossible to stand outside the continuous flux of events. As a traditional Scots Gaelic adage states:

"Ri traghad
's ri lionadh....
Mar a bha
Mar a tha
Mar a bhitheas
Gu brath
Ri tragadh
's ri lionadh".

(An English translation is,

"Ebbing and flowing....
As it was,
As it is,
As it shall be, evermore -
The ebb and the flow".)

Although they are necessary for everyday life to continue, all systems of classification must in some degree fail. There is a narrow line between using a system whilst recognizing its arbitrary nature, and taking it literally as a true description of reality, which is essentially only able to be experienced at first hand. This is understood in Bardo-Druidic teachings whose flexibility allows them to be practised in ways appropriate to any conditions that we may encounter.

All spiritual traditions are founded on a specific cognitive of one kind or another. People who possess a cognitive framework for their knowledge of existence on all its levels have a better chance of achieving their potential than those who have a chaotic world-view, for then they are chaotic within themselves. The nature of the Bardo-Druidic cognitive framework is expressed innately through the systems I describe in this book. Through them it is possible to gain access to the essentials of the inner wisdom of the Bardo-Druidic system of the British Isles, and to thereby to live creatively.

32. From the Emerald Table of Hermes Trismegistus.

# Appendices

These appendices contain information and correspondences essential to the understanding of Celtic Bardic 'alphabets'.

## List of Contents

*Appendix 1* is a full glossary of the terms used in *Ogham and Coelbren*.

*Appendix 2* gives Ogham correspondences as most commonly recognized by contemporary Oghamists.

*Appendix 3* gives a classification of Celtic tree-types from various ancient sources.

*Appendix 4* lists the Ogham names given by Roderick O'Flaherty in his *Ogygia* (1793).

*Appendix 5* lists the thirteen tree-months, as arranged by Robert Graves.

*Appendix 6* gives the correspondences between the *Feadha* of *An Ogham Craobh* and the divination cards of *The New Celtic Oracle* (Jackson and Pennick, 1997).

*Appendix 7* The Thirteen Precious Things of the Island of Britain.

*Appendix 8*. Division and measurement of time and space in the Welsh tradition.

*Appendix 9*. Bardo-Druidic chronology.

*Appendix 10*. The 22 constellations of Welsh traditional astronomy.

*Appendix 11*. The Bardic hierarchy.

*33. Etain, wife of Oghma Grianainech.*

# Appendix 1
# Glossary of Terms

| | |
|---|---|
| Abcedilros | the earliest British alphabet of ten letters (W). |
| Abred | the material world, Middle Earth (W). |
| Aibítir | alphabet (I). |
| Aicme | group of five Oghams (I). |
| Aird | one of the eight directions, place, family, homestead, attention, consciousness, presence (I). |
| Airt | Aird (q.v.) (S). |
| Aiteann | Furze (I). |
| Alba | the old Irish name for Scotland (I). |
| Alban Arthan | Winter Solstice (W) |
| Alban Eilir | Vernal Equinox (W). |
| Alban Elfed | Autumnal Equinox (W). |
| Alban Hefin | Summer Solstice (W). |
| Alraune | a magical root of Mandrake-type (Ge). |
| Annwn (Annwvyn) | the *lower world*, also known as *the loveless place, the land invisible*, and *the Abyss* (W). |
| An Ogham Craobh | the basic form of Ogham (I). |
| Anradh | chief poet of second order (I). |
| Anterth | The tide of *Vapourlessness* (7.30 - 10.30 AM) (W). |
| Ard Rí | the high king of Ireland (I). |
| Arris | the edge or corner of a dressed stone. |
| Awen | spirit, the power of inspiration; the Druidic threefold symbol of the divine spark (W). |

| | |
|---|---|
| Awenyddion | inspired poets or oracles (W). |
| Bannock | ceremonial biscuit or cake (S). |
| Bardd Teulu | court Bard, serving a lord (W). |
| Beltane | the May festival, starting at sunset on April 30 (C). |
| Beth-Luis-Nion | an alternative name for the Ogham 'alphabet' (I). |
| Beith | first letter of the Ogham alphabet (C). |
| Beith | Birch tree (I). |
| Bodhrán | Irish goat-skin drum. |
| Bore | Morningtide (W). |
| Brigantia | Candlemas, starting at sunset on January 31st (EP). |
| Broom-Cow | ceremonial besom of heather (S). |
| Burin | Tool for carving Oghams. (I). |
| Caledonia | the old name for the territory that became Scotland after the Scots (from Ireland) invaded and conquered it (L). |
| Caorthann | Rowan (Mountain Ash) tree (I). |
| Celyn | Holly (W) (see Cuileann). |
| Cerddorion | medieval minstrels (W). |
| Ceugant | the transcendent realm of the ineffable source (W). |
| Cláirseach | Irish harp (I). |
| Codi'r Fedwen | the Welsh ceremony of raising the Maypole (W). |
| Coelbren | letters carved onto wood (W). |
| Coelvain | letters carved onto stone (especially slate) (W). |
| Coll | Hazel tree (I). |
| Collen | Hazel tree (W). |
| Comraich | sacred enclosure around a holy place (eg. a church) (I). |
| Corrigan | elven spirit (B). |

| | |
|---|---|
| Crannog | artificial island on piles (such as a lake village) (W). |
| Craobh | 'bough', a line of Ogham characters (I). |
| Criafol | Rowan (W). |
| Croesaniaid | buffoons, fools, jesters, ribald rhymers (W). |
| Crossáin | buffoons, fools, jesters, satirists, ribald rhymers (I). |
| Cuileann | Holly tree (I). |
| Cymry | the Welsh people (W). |
| Cyntevin | the beginning of Summer (W). |
| Cyrven | letter burnt on wood by pyrography (W). |
| Cwywdd | Welsh poem in traditional metre (W). |
| Dair | Oak tree (I) (see Derwen). |
| Daronwy | "The Thunderer", by-name of God (W). |
| Dawns y Fedwen | Maypole dance (W). |
| Derwen | Oak tree (W). |
| Dewaint | the tide of midnight (W). |
| Draí | druid (I). |
| Draíon | Blackthorn (I). |
| Draoi | wizard (I). |
| Dreas | Bramble, see Sméar Dubh (I). |
| Druid | Pagan Celtic priest (OC). |
| Droim | 'line' on which Ogham characters are written (I). |
| Dumnonia | the old Celtic country covering the present counties of Devon and Cornwall in south-western England (Co). |
| Ebill (pl. Ebillion) | board or rod with letters (W). |
| Echwydd | The tide of Afternoon (1.30 - 4.30 PM) (W). |
| Eiddew | Ivy (W). |
| Eidhneán | Ivy (I). |
| Enhazelled | a field prepared for ritual combat by enclosing it with Hazel posts (E). |

| | |
|---|---|
| Fáistine | Prophecy (I). |
| Fasnacht (Fasnet) | the period of 'carnival' and 'misrule' leading up to Shrove Tuesday (Ge). |
| Feá | Beech tree (I). |
| Feisefín | Ogham wheel, otherwise 'Fionn's Wheel', 'Fionn's Window' or 'Fionn's Shield' (I). |
| Ffon Wen | 'the white stick', a Hazel rod used for insults (W). |
| Fidh (pl. Feadha) | a 'letter' in Ogham (I). |
| Fili | Irish poet (I). |
| Fleasc | a cut or line of an Ogham character (I). |
| Fleasc Filidh | Bardic wand (I). |
| Forfeada | 'Overtrees', the fifth *Aicme* of the Oghams (I). |
| Fraoch | Heather (I). |
| Fuinnseog | Ash tree (I). |
| Gaeilge | the indigenous Celtic language of Ireland (I). |
| Gael | an early medieval name for ethnic Irish people (including Scots) (I). |
| Gaelic | the Celtic language of Scotland (E). |
| Gall | an early medieval name for non-Irish (foreigners) (I). |
| Geis (pl. Geassa) | a magical prohibition, (taboo) (I). |
| Geranos | the Crane-Dance of the labyrinth (Gr). |
| Gheal | Hawthorn (Whitethorn) (I). |
| Ghuaim | wisdom (I). |
| Giolcach | Reed (I). |
| Giúis | Pine tree (I). |
| Gwechwydd | Eventide (W). |
| Gwyddoniaid | the men of letters, people endowed with reason and learning, i.e. Druids, Ovates or Bards (W). |
| Gruagach | an Otherworldly champion (I). |
| Gwyddbwll | a board game of the *tafl* group, which begins with a king at the centre, |

| | |
|---|---|
| | surrounded by his forces and besieged by opposing forces from the four quarters (W). |
| Gwynvyd | the spiritual upperworld, literally "the White Land" (W). |
| Holmganga | literally 'going on an island', ritual combat in a specially-delimited area (ON). |
| Hoslur | 'the Enhazelled Field', hazel-pole sacred enclosure for ritual combat (ON). |
| Iúr | Yew tree (I). |
| Kenning | poetic allusion, such as "horse of the sea" for ship (E). |
| Kvistrunar | 'twig-runes', a system of runic encryption resembling Ogham (ON). |
| Lammas | the first harvest, starting at sunset on July 31 (Lughnassadh, L'nasa (I)) (E). |
| Leamh–n | Elm tree (I). |
| Leamh–n bog | Hornbeam tree (lit. soft Elm) (I). |
| Limewood | wod of the Linden Tree (Tilia *platyphyllos*) (E). |
| List | fenced area used in tournaments and medieval ritual combat. |
| Litir | a character in the Gaelic *Aibítir* (I). |
| Llan | sacred enclosure around a holy place (eg. a church, c.f. Comraich) (W). |
| Llythrau | letters cut on wood, from Welsh *Lly*, what is manifest, and *Tyr* to cut. |
| Lunantishee | guardian sprite of the Blackthorn (Straif) (I). |
| Manred | "the flowing particles" - the basic constituent of matter (W). |

| | |
|---|---|
| May Tree | Whitethorn (*Crataegus monogyna*) (E). |
| May Tree | Maypole (E). |
| Mete-Wand | measuring-stick (in Irish context, a rod for measuring the dead) (E). |
| Modor | by-name of God (the power, from which the English 'motor') (W). |
| Muime | mythological monster from Scandinavia that destroyed the Wood of Caledon in Scotland (S). |
| Narrenbaum | 'fools' tree', the pole erected at Fasnacht (Shrovetide) in south Germany (G). |
| Narrenzunft | fools' guild (G). |
| Nawn | Noontide (W). |
| Nemeton | sanctuary, often a sacred grove of trees (C). |
| Nimidas | the "ceremonies of the woodland" (Ga). |
| Nodaighe | 'certain abbreviations' in medieval Irish cryptography (I). |
| Nwyf | energy (W), (see Nwyvre). |
| Nwyvre | the *quintessence*, viewed as the vital breath or Universal Soul, equivalent to the önd of the Norse (W). |
| Ogham (Ogam) | (pronounced o'om), the Celtic tree-alphabet (I). |
| Oíche Shamhna | Hallowe'en/All Saints' Day (see Samhain) (I). |
| Ollamh | literally, 'supreme' or 'most transcendent', master-poet (Chief Poet of the First Order) of Ireland. A title once used for the chief of every hierarchy (I). |
| Omphalos | literally, the *navel of the world*, a central place of assembly and oracles (see Nowl) (Gr). |
| Onnen | Ash tree (W). |

| | |
|---|---|
| Peithenyn | wooden frame holding wooden bars with writing (W). |
| Peithynvain | 'the stones of elucidation', Welsh Bardic stone tablets (W). |
| Pencerdd | chief Bard "who has won a competition for a chair" (W). |
| Pill | splinter (W). |
| Pillwydd | wooden bar with letters (W). |
| Pisky | a Cornish sprite (Co). |
| Plagawd | an ancient form of paper, made from a sedge or Papyrus believed to be imported to Britain from India by the Romans (W). |
| Pobail | Poplar tree (I). |
| Pobail Ban | Aspen tree (I). |
| Pren | wood (old Welsh) (W). |
| Pylgeint | Dawn (W). |
| Rhabdomancy | divining for water or metal, using a rod (E). |
| Rhabdomant | a practitioner of Rhabdomancy (E). |
| Rune | character in the Germanic/Norse magical alphabet (Ge)(E). |
| Sailéach | Willow tree (I). |
| Samhain | (pronounced sow'ain), a modern English Pagan name for the old Celtic festival that included Samhnag, Lá Samhna and Oíche Shamhna, Christianized as Holymas/All Saints' Day, the beginning of the old Celtic year, commencing at sunset on October 31 (I). (see Oíche Shamhna). |
| Scotia | ancient name for Ireland (I). |
| Scriptorium | monastic scribes' office (L). |
| Shrovetide | the days leading up to Shrove Tuesday (E). |
| Sméar Dubh | Blackberry ( q.v. Dreas) (I). |

| | |
|---|---|
| Spíonán | Gooseberry (I). |
| | |
| Tabhall Lorga | tablet-staff, symbol of office of Bards (I). |
| Taibhli Fileadh | 'Tables of the Poets' (I). |
| Tamlorga Filidh | 'Staves of the Poets' (I). |
| Tarngaireacht | divination (I). |
| Temenos | sacred enclosure around a temple (Gr). |
| Trom | Elder tree (I). |
| Troslathau | connecting Pillwydd (q.v.). |
| | |
| Ucher | Overcast (tide from 7.30 - 10.30 PM) (W). |
| | |
| Vatis | Pagan Celtic diviner (Ga). |
| Vébond | sacred enclosure with Hazel posts linked by rope (ON). |
| | |
| Walpurgisnacht | May Eve (G). |
| Whitethorn | Hawthorn or May Tree (*Crataegus monogyna: Huath*) (E). |
| | |
| Y Fedwen Haf | the Summer Birch (midsummer pole) (W). |
| Y Gangen Haf | the Summer Branch (W). |
| Yries | Gaulish spirit-paths or "Pagan Trackways", marked by rags, shoes or other votive offerings (Ga). |

Key to abbreviations:

| | | | | |
|---|---|---|---|---|
| B | Breton. | | C | Continental Celtic. |
| Co | Cornish. | | E | traditional English. |
| Ga | Gaulish. | | Ge | German. |
| Gr | Greek. | | I | Irish. |
| L | Latin. | | ON | Old Norse. |
| S | Scots. | | W | Welsh. |

# Appendix 2

Ogham Correspondences as most commonly recognized. Bird Ogham only applies to the first twenty *Feadha*.

**1. The *Aicme* of Beith (BLFSN)**

| Name | Roman | Tree | Bird Name | | Colour |
|---|---|---|---|---|---|
| Beith | B | Birch | Besan | Pheasant | White |
| Luis | L | Rowan | Lachu | Duck | Grey |
| Fearn | F | Alder | Faelinn | Gull | Crimson |
| Saille | S | Willow | Seg | Hawk | Bright (beautiful) |
| Nuin | N | Ash | Naescu | Snipe | Clear |

**2. The *Aicme* of Huath (HDTCQ)**

| Name | Roman | Tree | Bird Name | | Colour |
|---|---|---|---|---|---|
| Huath | H | Hawthorn | Hadaig | Crow | Terrible (Purple) |
| Duir | D | Oak | Droem | Wren | Black |
| Tinne | T | Holly | Truith | Starling | Grey-Green |
| Coll | C | Hazel | Corr | Crane | Brown |
| Quert | Q | Apple | Querc | Chicken | Green |

## 3. The *Aicme* of Muin (MGNgStR)

| Name | Roman | Tree | Bird Name | Colour |
|---|---|---|---|---|
| Muin | M | Vine | Mintan Titmouse | Multi-coloured |
| Gort | G | Ivy | Géis Mute Swan | Blue |
| Ngetal | Ng | Reed | Ngéigh Goose | Grass Green |
| Straif | St | Blackthorn | Stmolach Thrush | Purple-Black |
| Ruis | R | Elder | Rócnat Rook | Blood-Red |

## 4. The *Aicme* of Ailm (AOUEI)

| Name | Roman | Tree | Bird Name | Colour |
|---|---|---|---|---|
| Ailm | A | Elm (Fir) | Aidhircléog Lapwing | Black-white |
| On | O | Furze | Odorscrach Cormorant | Dun |
| Ur | U | Heather | Uiséog Lark | Purple |
| Edadh | E | Aspen | Ela Swan | Fox-red |
| Ida | I | Yew | Illait Eaglet | White |

## 5. The *Forfeadha* or the *Aicme* of Eabhadh (EaOiUiIoAi)

| Name | Roman | Tree | Colour |
|---|---|---|---|
| Eabhadh | EA | Aspen | Green |
| Oir | OI | Spindle | White |
| Uinllean | UI | Honeysuckle | Tawny |
| Ifin | IO | Gooseberry | White |
| Amancholl | AI | Pine | (Rainbow) |

# Appendix 3
# Classification of Celtic Tree Types

The *Book of Ballymote* lists the following:
Royal or Chieftain Trees (8): Elm, Oak, Hazel, Vine, Ivy, Blackthorn, Broom, Spindle.
Kiln or Peasant Trees (8): Birch, Rowan, Willow, Ash, Whitethorn, Fig, Apple, Cork.
Spiral or Green Trees (8): not listed.

The *Auraicept na nÉces* states:
"How many groups of Oghams? Three: namely eight Chieftain Trees and eight Peasants' Trees and seven bushes:
Eight Chieftain Trees: first Alder, Oak, Hazel, Vine, Ivy, Blackthorn. Gorse, Heather: Eight Peasant Trees, namely: Birch, Rowan. Willow, Ash, Whitethorn, Broom, Holly, Apple. After their letters, all other bushes are Bush Trees."

Traditional Irish *Brehon Law* (IV, 147) lists seven Chieftain Trees, seven Peasant Trees, seven Shrub Trees and eight Bushes.
Chieftain Trees: Dair (Oak), Coll (Hazel), Cuileann (Holly), Ibur (Yew), Iundius (Ash), Ochtach (Fir), Aball (Apple).
Peasant Trees: Fernn (Alder), Sail (Willow), Scaith (Whitethorn), Caerthann (Rowan), Beithe (Birch), Leam (Elm), Idha (Ivy).
Shrub Trees: Draidean (Blackthorn), Trom (Elder), Fincoll (White Hazel), Crithach (Aspen), Caithne (Strawberry Tree),

Feorus (uncertain), Crann-Fir (uncertain).
Eight Bushes: Raith (Fern), Rait (uncertain), Aiteand (Gorse), Dris (Dog Rose), Freach (Heather), Eideand (uncertain), Gilcoch (Broom), Spin (Spindle).

# Appendix 4

Ogham Names given by Roderick O'Flaherty in his *Ogygia* (Dublin, 1793).

B  Boibel
L  Loth
F  Forann
N  Neiagadon
S  Salia
H  Uiria
D  Daibhaith
T  Teilmon
C  Caoi
Q  (CC) Cailep
M  Moiria
G  Gath
Ng Ngoimar
Y  Ydra
R  Rieuben
A  Acab
O  Ose
U  Ura
E  Esu
I  Jaichin

# Appendix 5
# The Tree-Months
## (After Robert Graves)

In his *The White Goddess*, Robert Graves put together the Ogham *Feadha* with a thirteen 'month' calendar that he derived from 'the voice of God' in *The Song of Amergin*. Although there is little historical precedence for this, it has proved very popular, and has become an integral part of contemporary Celtic and Goddess spirituality. In certain places in the British Isles and on mainland Europe, circular groves of these thirteen Ogham trees have been planted as places of spiritual power.

| Tree Month | Dates | Ogham letter |
|---|---|---|
| Birchmoon | 24 Dec - 20 Jan | Beth (Beith) |
| Rowanmoon | 21 Jan - 17 Feb | Luis |
| Ashmoon | 18 Feb - 17 Mar | Nion (Nin) |
| Aldermoon | 18 Mar - 14 Apr | Fearn |
| Willowmoon | 15 Apr - 12 May | Saille |
| Hawthornmoon | 13 May - 9 Jun | Huath |
| Oakmoon | 10 Jun - 7 Jul | Duir |
| Hollymoon | 8 Jul - 4 Aug | Tinne |
| Hazelmoon | 5 Aug - 1 Sep | Coll |
| Bramblemoon | 2 Sep - 29 Sep | Muin |
| Ivymoon | 30 Sep - 27 Oct | Gort |
| Reedmoon | 28 Oct - 24 Nov | Ngetal |
| Eldermoon | 25 Nov - 22 Dec | Ruis |
| Secret of the Unhewn Dolmen | 23 Dec | ---- |

# Appendix 6
# The Oghams and The New Celtic Oracle

Meanings and correspondences of the cards of *The New Celtic Oracle* (Nigel Jackson and Nigel Pennick, Capall Bann 1997) In this divination-card system, reversed cards have the opposite meaning to upright ones. The meaning of the White Roebuck does not change whichever way up it comes.

| Ogham | Card Name | Interpretation |
|---|---|---|
| Beth | The Birch Tree | coming changes, new things, growth |
| Luis | The Lady of the Unicorn | guarding power, stimulus, creativity |
| Nion | The World Tree | communication, awareness, new influences |
| Fearn | The Wondrous Head | openness, inner voices, youth |
| Saille | The Hawk of May | clear views, awakening abilities, flexibility |
| Huath | The Flower Maiden | life, active forces, new possibilities |
| Duir | The Oak King | will-power, courage, strength, certainty |

| | | |
|---|---|---|
| Tinne | The Green Knight | challenges, tests, ordeals |
| Coll | The Nuts of Wisdom | understanding, inspiration. |
| Quert | The Island of Apples | healing, recovery, regeneration |
| Muin | The Harvest Vine | rest, renewal, fruits of labours |
| Gort | The Ivy Bush | stormy times, success despite problems |
| Ngetal | The Wild Hunt | a threat, unavoidable change |
| Straif | The Increaser of Secrets | attacks, struggles, conflict |
| Ruis | The Daughter of the Bones | breaking-down, difficulties |
| Ailim | The Lapwing | concealed new beginnings, secrecy |
| Onn | The Queen of the East | new opportunities |
| Ur | The Summer Queen | personal success, well-being |
| Eadha | The Queen of the West | sensitivity |
| Iodho | The Weaving Sisters | powerful influences, inevitable things |
| | The Sword of Nuada | enlightenment |
| | The Spear of Lugh | inner strength |
| | The Cauldron of the Dagda | passive emotions |
| | The Stone of Destiny | truth, honour, order, justice |
| | The White Roebuck | secret spiritual impulses |

# Appendix 7
# The Thirteen Precious Things of the Island of Britain

These magical objects from Welsh mythology can be related to the thirteen Oghams of the year-cycle. They are:

B. The Sword of Dyrnwyn of Rhydderch Hael, which only he could draw.
L. The Hamper of Gwyddno Garanhir, which multiplied the food put in it one hundredfold.
F. The Horn of Bran Galed, which contained whatever drink the drinker desired.
S. The Chariot of Morgan Mwynvawr, which magically transported anyone wherever they wanted to go.
N. The Halter of Clyno Eiddyn, which would find any horse he wished to ride.
H. The Knife of Llawfrodded Farchawg, which simultaneously served two dozen men their meat.
D. The Cauldron of Tyrnog which boiled meat only for the brave.
T. The Whetstone of Tudwal Tudclud, which sharpened only the swords of the brave.
C. The Coat of Padarn Beisrudd, which fitted only a nobleman, never a peasant.
Q/M. The Plate of Rhegynydd Ysgolhaig, which, along with

165

the eleventh Precious Thing, the Pan, found whatever food one requested.

G. The Golden Gwyddbwll Gameboard of Gwenddolen, whose playing-pieces made of silver played a game by themselves.

Ng. The Cloak of Arthur, which made the wearer invisible.

# Appendix 8
# Time and Space in the Welsh Tradition

In the Welsh tradition, the Nadir, or lowest point (beneath the Earth, and hence marked by the central point or *omphalos*) is called *Isafbwynt*. The highest point, the Zenith directly overhead is called *Entrych* or *Anterth*. East, the rising direction of the sun, is *Dwyrain*; South is called *Deau* or *De*; West is *Gorllewin*; and North is *Gogledd*. In common with the other northern European cultures, Celtic tradition divides the day into eight tides of three hours apiece. In traditional societies, before the invention of mechanical clocks and time zones, time was told by the position of the sun in the day, and by the stars at night. Thus, a time corresponds with a direction.

The entire cycle of the Welsh eight tides is *Dewaint* (Midnight), which runs from 10.30 PM until 1.30 AM; *Pylgeint* (Dawning), from 1.30 AM until 4.30; *Bore* (Morningtide), lasting from 4.30 until 7.30; and *Anterth* (The Tide of Vapourlessness), beginning at 7.30 and ending at 10.30. The tide of *Nawn* (Noontide) runs from 10.30 AM until 1.30 PM. *Nawn* is followed by *Echwydd* (Rest), from 1.30 until 4.30 PM. Next comes *Gwechwydd* (Eventide or Twilight), whose period extends from 4.30 until 7.30. The final tide is *Ucher* (Overcast or Disappearance), which runs from 7.30 until 10.30, when it is followed by *Dewaint*. According to tradition, these tides are at their greatest strength at their middle. Thus in the Welsh tradition, the times of *Nawn* (midday) and *Dewaint* (midnight) fall at the middle of their respective tides.

# Appendix 9
# Bardo-Druidic Chronology

British (Welsh) traditional chronology begins with Prydain, son of Aedd Mawr (Aedd the Great), in 480 BCE. Therefore 2000 CE is 2480 EP in the Prydain Calendar.

Bardic tradition recognizes three divisions of the year: The time of Summer, from *Cyntevin* to the Calend of October (October 1); Winter, from the Calend of October, to the Calend of February (February 1); and Spring, from the Calend of February to *Cyntevin*. The First day of *Cyntevin* is the beginning of Summer. It is equivalent to March 9 Old Style (March 10, O.S. in church computation, and March 20 in the contemporary Gregorian Calendar). *Cyntevin* proper runs until the summer solstice Alban Hevin, after which summer proper commenced.

*John Jones's Almanack* (1752), states that before the days of Prydain, the year began at *Alban Arthan*, December 9, O.S.. According to the *Book of Tre'rbryn*, there are four quarter days called the Albans ('primary points' or 'stations of the Sun') in the Bardo-Druidic year: *Alban Elved* is the calend of October; *Alban Arthan* is the calend of January; *Alban Eilir* is the calend of Spring; and *Alban Hevin* is the calend of Summer. Traditionally, the four 'Stations of the Sun' are : The point of roughness (*Alban Arthan*) (winter solstice); The point of regeneration (*Alban Eilir*) (vernal equinox); The point of

169

summer (*Alban Hefin*) (summer solstice); The point of reaping time (*Alban Elfed*) (autumnal equinox).

The Celtic tradition preserved in Irish, Scottish and English farmers' calendars recognizes four 'Fire Festivals' in addition to the four Quarter Days. They divide the year into eight, the *Ogdoadic Year*. Beginning at the Winter Solstice, the first festival is the Welsh *Alban Arthan*, English *Yule* and the old Scots *Hogmanay*. Next comes Imbolc (Brigantia, Oimelc, Candlemas, 1 - 2 February), then the Vernal Equinox (22-23 March, Welsh, *Alban Eilir*). This is followed by May Day (Lá Béalteine (I), Beltaine, Beltane), then the Summer Solstice (*Alban Hefin*, St John's Day, St Jean (Breton)). After this, on the Calends of August (August 1) is Lammas (Lughnassadh, Lá Lúnasa), the harvest festival of the first loaf. Next comes the Autumnal Equinox (September 22-23), *Alban Elfed*. The final festival of the cycle (which is the Celtic new year) is Samhain (Oíche Shamhna, Lá Samhna, Allhallows' Eve, Hallowe'en), and the wheel turns round again.

# Appendix 10
# Welsh Traditional Astronomy: The Thirty-Seven Constellations.

According to Bardo-Druidic tradition, there are seven visible 'planets', and eight others which are invisible. The seven 'planets' are those customary in Western traditional astrology: the Sun, the Moon, Mercury, Venus, Mars, Jupiter and Saturn. According to tradition, usually one cannot see the other eight. They appear only at certain points of a very long time cycle, so they may be notable comets according to modern understanding. In addition to the visible and occult planets, traditional Welsh astronomers recognized a number of constellations which they named after individuals and things in Celtic legendary history and mythology.

As the Primary Bard of Britain, Taliesin, tells us in *Hanes Taliesin*: "I know the names of all of the stars from the north to the south .... I have been three times in Caer Arianrhod .... I obtained my inspiration from the Cauldron of Ceridwen .... I have been in an uneasy chair above Caer Sidi, and the whirling round without motion between three elements". (Constellations 1, 25 and 16). The *Gower Wassail* from south Wales refers to astronomical correctness:

"We know by the Moon
That we are not too soon.....

We know by the stars
That we are not too far..."

In most cases, the Welsh constellations do not correspond with those of classical Graeco-Arabic astronomy, nor to the Anglo-Saxon and Norse constellations as described by Otto Sigfrid Reuter in his *Germanische Himmelskunde* (1934). In the Welsh tradition, the stars are arranged in the following 37 groupings (English translation and correspondence, where direct, in brackets):

1. Caer Arianrhod (The City of Arianrhod, *Corona Borealis*).
2. Yr Orsedd Wenn (The White Throne).
3. Telyn Arthur (Arthur's Harp, *Lyra*).
4. Caer Gwydion (The City of Gwydion - the Galaxy).
5. Yr Haeddel fawr (The Great Plough-tail, *Ursa Major*).
6. Yr Haeddel fach (The Little Plough-tail - *Ursa Minor*).
7  Y Long fawr (The Great Ship).
8. Y Long foel (The Bald Ship).
9. Y Llatheidan (The Yard - *Orion*).
10. Y Twr Tewdws (Theodosius's Group  - *The Pleiades*).
11. Y Tryfelan (The Triangle).
12. Llys Don (Don's Palace - *Cassiopeia*).
13. Llwyn Blodeuwedd (Blodeuwedd's Grove).
14. Cadair Teyrnon (Teyrnon's Chair).
15. Caer Eiddionydd (The City of Eiddionydd).
16. Caer Sidi (The City of Sidi - the *ecliptic*).
17. Cwlwm Cancaer (The Conjunction of a Hundred Circles).
18. Lluest Elmur (Elmur's Camp).
19. Bwa'r Milwr (The Soldier's Bow).
20. Brynn Dinan (Dinan's Hill).
21. Nyth yr Eryres (The She-Eagle's Nest).
22. Trosol Bleiddyd (Bladud's Lever).
23. Asgell y Gwynt (The Wind's Wing).
24. Y Feillionen (The Trefoil).
25. Pair Ceridwen (Ceridwen's Cauldron).
26. Dolen Teifi (Teifi's Bend).

27. Yr Esgair fawr (The Great Limb).
28. Yr Esgair fechan (The Little Limb).
29. Y Ychen Bannog (The Large-Horned Oxen - *Gemini*).
30. Y Maes mawr (The Great Plain).
31. Y fforch wenn (The White Fork).
32. Y Baedd Coed (The Woodland Boar).
33. Llywethan (The Muscle).
34. Yr Hebog (The Hawk).
35. March Llyr (Llyr's Horse).
36. Cadair Elffin (Elffin's Chair).
37. Neuadd Olwen (Olwen's Hall).

# Appendix 11
# The Bardic Hierarchy

In Welsh tradition, the chief Bard, "who has won a competition for a chair" is called *Pencerdd*. In Irish society, this rank was paralleled by the *Ollamh* (Chief *Fili*). Next in precedence below the *Pencerdd* comes the *Bardd Teulu*, a court Bard whose symbol of office was a harp given to him by his lord, with which he must never part. He sang to the warriors before a raid, and sang *The Monarchy of Britain* to them before a battle. The lower-ranking Bards are the *Cerddorion* (minstrels) and, below them, the *Croesaniaid* (buffoons, fools and ribald rhymers). The use of the *Ffon Wen* may be a continuation of the practices of the *Croesaniaid*.

This lowest rank appears to be equivalent to the Irish *Crosáin*, who went around in bands. There is an ancient Irish account of nine such "black and hairy" figures who chanted all night on the fresh grave of a dead king. They were expelled by Christian priests at dawn. Linked to these were the satirists (who have their parallel in the contemporary *Schandtle* of the Schwäbisch-alemannischer Fasnacht). The ancient laws of Ireland called them "the sons of death and bad men", and ranked them among "fools, jesters, buffoons, outlaws, heathens and harlots, who hold demon banquets".

# Bibliography

Abbott, M: *Green Woodwork - Working with Wood the Natural Way.* Guild of Master Craftsmen, London, 1989.
Ab Ithell, J. Williams: *Barddas; or, a Collection of Original Documents, illustrative of the Theology, Wisdom and Usages of the Bardo-Druidic System of the Isle of Britain.* 2 vols.,The Welsh Mss. Society, Llandovery, 1866.
Anderson, J.: *Scotland in Pagan Times.* David Douglas, Edinburgh, 1868.
Anon: *Ornamental Irish Antiquities.* Waterhouse & Co., Dublin, 1852.
Anon (His Majesty's Commissioners): *The Royal Commission on the Ancient Monuments of Scotland. Twelfth Report with an Inventory of the Ancient Monuments of Orkney & Shetland. Volume III. Inventory of Shetland.* H.M.S.O., Edinburgh, 1946.
Anwyl, Edward: *Celtic Religion.* Archibald Constable, London, 1906.
Anwyl, Edward: *Ancient Celtic Goddesses.* The Celtic Review III (1907)
Arntz, Helmut: 'Das Ogom'. *Beiträge zur Geschichte des deutsche Sprache und Literatur,* 59, 321-413 (1935).
Atkinson, R. (ed.): *The Book of Leinster.* Oxford University Press, Oxford, 1880.
Auld, William Muir: *Christmas.* Macmillan, London, 1931.
Bamford, Christopher, & Marsh, William Price: *Celtic Christianity.* Floris Books, Edinburgh, 1986.
Baring, A., & Cashford, J.: *The Myth of the Goddess.* Book Club Associates, London, 1993.
Baring-Gould, S.: *A Book of Devon.* Methuen, London 1909.
Baring-Gould, S., & Fisher, J.: *The Lives of the British Saints.* Honourable Society of Cymmrodorion, London, 1907.
Bärtsch, Albert: *Holz Masken, Fastnachts- und Maskenbrauchtum in der Schweiz, in Sıddeutschland uns Österreich.* AT Verlag, Aarau, 1993.
Binchy, D. A.: 'The Fair of Tailtu and the Feast of Tara'. Eriu XVIII (1958).
Blake, Lois: *Traditional Dance and Customs in Wales.* Llangollen, 1972.
Bonwick, J.: *Irish Druids and Old Irish Religions.* London, 1894.
Bossert, Helmuth T.: *Folk Art of Europe.* A. Zwemmer, London, 1954.
Bötticher, Carl: *Der Baumkultus der Hellenen.* Berlin, 1856.
Bowen, Dewi: *Ancient Siluria.* Llanerch, Felinfach, 1992.
Bowen, E.G.: *The Settlements of the Celtic Saints in Wales.* University of Wales Press, Cardiff, 1956.

Breathnach, Breandan: *Folk Music and Dances of Ireland*. Mercier, Dublin, 1986.
Brekilien, Yann: *La Mythologie Celtique*. Editions Jean Picollec, Paris, 1981.
Broadwood, Lucy E., and Maitland, J.A. Fuller: *English County Songs*. Leadenhall Press, London, 1893.
Brosse, Jacques: *Mythologie des Arbres*. Plon, Paris, 1989.
Bromwich, R.: *Trioedd Ynys Prydein: The Welsh Triads*. University of Wales Press, Cardiff, 1979.
Brown, Theo: *The Fate of the Dead: Folk Eschatology in the West Country After the Reformation*. D.S. Brewer, Cambridge, 1979.
Brunaux, Jean Louis: *The Celtic Gauls: Gods, Rites and Sanctuaries*. Seaby, London, 1988.
Bryce, Derek: *Symbolism of the Celtic Cross*. Gomer, Llandyssul, 1989.
Bucknell, Peter A.: *Entertainment and Ritual 600 - 1600*. Stainer & Bell, London, 1979.
Byrne, Patrick F.: *Witchcraft in Ireland*. Mercier, Cork, 1967.
Calder, George (trans. and ed.): *Auraicept na nÉces, The Scholar's Primer*. John Grant, Edinburgh, 1917.
Campbell, J.G.: *Superstitions of the Highlands and Islands of Scotland*. Edinburgh, 1900.
Carmichael, Alexander: *Carmina Gaedelica*. Scottish Academic Press, Edinburgh, 1940.
Cawte, E.C.: *Ritual Animal Disguise*. D.S. Brewer, Cambridge, 1978.
Chadwick, N.K.: *Poetry and Prophecy*. Cambridge University Press, Cambridge, 1942.
Christian, Roy: *Old English Customs*. David & Charles, Newton Abbot, 1974.
Clarus, Ingeborg: *Keltische Mythen: der Mensch und seine Anderswelt*. Walter, Olten, 1991.
Close-Brooks, J., & Stevenson, R.B.K.: *Dark Age Sculpture*. Royal Commission on Historic Monuments, Edinburgh, 1982.
Condren, Mary: *The Serpent and the Goddess: Women, Religion and Power in Celtic Ireland*, Harper & Row, San Francisco, 1989.
Cooper, Emmanuel: *People's Art*. Mainstream Publishing, Edinburgh & London, 1994.
Cross, T. P., & Slover, C. H.: *Ancient Irish Tales*. Dublin, 1969.
Crossing, William: *The Ancient Stone Crosses of Dartmoor and its Borderland*. Exeter, 1902.
Cubbon, M.: *The Art of Manx Crosses*. The Manx Museum and National Trust, Douglas, 1971.
Cunnack, Edward M.: *The Helston Furry Dance*. The Flora Day Association and the Stewards of the Helston Furry Dance, Helston, 1968.
Daniell, S.: *Old Cornwall*. Tor Mark Press, Truro, n.d.
Dannheimer, Hermann, & Gebhard, Rupert: *Das keltische Jahrtausend*. Verlag Philipp Von Zabern, Mainz, 1993.

Darkstar, Erynn: *Ogham, Tree-Lore and The Celtic Tree Oracle. 1: Searching for Roots.* Manteia 3 (1990), 29 - 31.
Darkstar, Erynn: *Ogham, Tree-Lore and The Celtic Tree Oracle. Searching for Roots*, Part 2. Manteia 4 (1990), 32 - 35.
Darkstar, Erynn: *Ogham, Tree-Lore and The Celtic Tree Oracle. Searching for Roots*, Part 3. Manteia 6 (1991), 22 - 25.
Darkstar, Erynn: *Ogham, Tree-Lore and The Celtic Tree Oracle. Searching for Roots*, Part 3 (cont.). Manteia 7 (1992), 22 - 24.
Davidson, Hilda Ellis: *Myths and Symbols in Pagan Europe: Early Scandinavian and Celtic Religions.* Manchester University Press, Manchester, 1988.
Davies, J.C.: *Folk-lore in West and Mid-Wales.* University of Wales Press, Aberystwyth, 1911.
Davies, Wendy: *Wales in the Early Middle Ages.* Leicester University Press, Leicester, 1982.
Deeney, D.: *Peasant Lore from Gaelic Ireland.* London, 1901.
Denyer, Susan: *Traditional Buildings and Life in the Lake District.* Victor Gollancz/ Peter Crawley, London, 1991.
de Paor, Máire & de Paor, Liam: *Early Christian Ireland.* Thames & Hudson, London, 1958.
de Vries, Jan: *Keltische Religion.* Kohlhammer, Stuttgart, 1961.
Dillon, Myles: *Early Irish Literature.* University of Chicago Press, Chicago, 1948.
Dillon, Myles (ed. & trans.):*'The Taboos of the Kings of Ireland'.* Proceedings of the Royal Irish Academy LIV (1951).
Dillon, Myles & Chadwick, Nora K.: *The Celtic Realms.* Cardinal, London, 1973.
Dinneen, Patrick S.: *Focloir Gaedhlige agus Bearla.* Dublin, 1927.
Dontenville, H.: *La Mythologie francaise.* Paris, 1948.
Drake-Carnell, F. J.: *Old English Customs and Ceremonies.* Batsford, London, 1938.
Dumézil, Georges: *Les Dieux des indo-européens. Mythes et réligions*, Paris, 1952.
Ellis, Peter Berresford: *Dictionary of Irish Mythology.* Constable, London, 1989.
Ellis, Peter Berresford: *Dictionary of Celtic Mythology.* Constable, London, 1992.
Ellis, T.P.: *Welsh Tribal Law and Custom.* Oxford University Press, Oxford, 1926.
Evans, E. Estyn: *Irish Folk Ways.* Routledge & Kegan Paul, London, 1957.
Evans, J.G. (ed.): *The Black Book of Carmarthen.* Pwllheli, 1906.
Evans, J.G. (ed.): *The Book of Taliesin.* Llanbedrog, 1910.
Evans, J.G. (ed.): *The Poetry from the Red Book of Hergest.* Llanbedrog, 1911.
Evans-Wentz, W.Y.: *The Fairy Faith in Celtic Countries.* Oxford University Press, Oxford, 1911.

Favyn, A.: *A Theatre of Honour and Knighthood.* London, 1623.
Fell, Barry: *'Windmill Hill Amulets'.* Epigraphic Society Occasional Publications, vol. 15 (1986).
Fischer, Susanne: *Blätter von Bäumen, Legenden, Mythen, Heilanwendung und Betrachtung von einheimischen Bäumen.* Heldenwang, 1980.
Fitzpatrick, Jim: *Erinsaga.* Dé Danaan Press, Dublin, 1985.
Frampton, George: *Grovely! Grovely! and all Grovely! The History of Oak Apple Day in Great Wishford.* York, 1992.
Gantz, J.: *The Mabinogion.* Penguin, Harmondsworth, 1976.
Gantz, J.: *Early Irish Myths and Sagas.* Penguin, London, 1981.
Geraldus Cambrensis (Gerald of Wales, trans. Thorpe, Lewis): *The Journey Through Wales / The Description of Wales.* Penguin, London, 1978.
Gercke, Hans (ed.): *Der Baum in Mythologie, Kunstgeschichte und Gegenwartskunst.* Heidelberg, 1985.
Gerschel, L.: *'Origine et premier usage des caractères Ogamiques'.* Ogam IX (1959), 151-173.
Graham, Frank: *Old Inns & Taverns of Yorkshire* (North Riding). V. Graham, Newcastle-upon-Tyne, 1965.
Graves, Robert: *The White Goddess.* Faber, London, 1961.
Green, M.: *The Gods of the Celts.* Alan Sutton, Gloucester, 1986.
Green, M.: *Symbol and Image in Celtic Religious Art.* Routledge, London, 1989.
Gregory, Lady: *Cuchulain of Muirthemne.* John Murray, London, 1911.
Grinsell, L.V.: *Folklore of Prehistoric Sites in Britain.* David and Charles, Newton Abbot, 1976.
Guénon, René: *Le Roi du Monde.* Paris, 1927.
Guyonvarc'h, Christian J.: *Textes mythologiques irlandais.* Ogam-Celticum, Nantes, 1981.
Gwynn, E. (ed. & trans.): *The Metrical Dindschenchas.* Todd Lecture Series IX, Part 2 (1906).
Hardy, P.D.: *The Holy Wells of Ireland.* Dublin, 1836.
Harte, Frank (ed.): *Songs of Dublin.* Ossian Publications, Cork, 1993.
Harte, Jeremy: *Herne the Hunter - A Case of Mistaken Identity?* At The Edge No. 3, 1996, 27 - 33.
Hartmann, Hans: *Der totenkult in Irland.* Freiburg, 1969.
Hatt, J.J.: *The Ancient Civilization of the Celts and Gallo-Romans.* London, 1970.
Helm, Alex: *The Mummers' Play.* D.S. Brewer, Ipswich, 1981.
Henderson, G.: *Survivals in Belief among the Celts.* Glasgow: James Maclehose and Sons, Glasgow, 1911.
Herbert, Henri: *'Le Mythe d'Epona', Mélanges linguistiques oferts ' M.j. Vendreyes,* Paris, 1935.
Herrick, Robert: *The Poems of Robert Herrick* (1648). Grant Richards, London, 1902.
Hesse, Hermann: *Bäume.* Insel, Frankfurt-Main, 1984.

Hetmann, Frederik (ed.). *Irischer Zaubergärten*. Fischer, Frankfurt, 1984.
Hetmann, Frederik: *Baum und Zauber*. Goldmann, Munich, 1988.
Hogan, Eileen: *Ogham: Each Letter of the Alphabet is Presented With a Colour and a Bird*. Burnt Wood Press, London, 1978.
Howell, James: *Dodona's Grove*. London, 1644.
Hughes, A. Lloyd: *The Welsh Folk Museum Manuscripts*. Folklife 17, (1979).
Hull, E.: *Cuchulain*. London, 1911.
Hutton, Ronald: *The Rise and Fall of Merrie England*. Oxford University Press, Oxford, 1994.
Hutton, Ronald: *The Stations of the Sun. A History of the Ritual Year In Britain*. Oxford University Press, Oxford, 1996.
Jackson, Kenneth H.A.: *A Celtic Miscellany*. Routledge and Kegan Paul, London, 1951.
Jackson, Kenneth H.A.: *Notes on the ogham inscriptions of southern Britain*. In Fox, C. & Bruce-Dickins (eds.) *Early Cultures of North-Western Europe*. London, 1950.
Jackson, Kenneth H.A.: *Language and History in Early Britain*. Edinburgh, 1953.
Jackson, Nigel: *Masks of Misrule - The Horned God and his Cult in Europe*. Capall Bann, Chieveley, 1995.
Jackson, Nigel: *Call of the Horned Piper*. Capall Bann, Chieveley, 1995.
Jackson, Nigel, & Pennick, Nigel: *The New Celtic Oracle*. Capall Bann, Chieveley, 1997.
Jacobsthal, P.: *Early Celtic Art*. Oxford University Press, Oxford, 1944.
James, David (compiler and editor): *Celtic Arts and Crafts Planetary Directory 1999*. Celtic Connections, Portesham, 1999.
James, E.: *Seasonal Feasts and Festivals*. London, Thames and Hudson, London, 1961.
Jensen, K. Frank: *The Prophetic Cards - a catalog of cards for fortune-telling*. Ouroboros, Roskilde, 1985.
Jensen, K. Frank: *The Prophetic Cards 2 - 110 more fortune-telling decks*. Ouroboros, Roskilde, 1990.
Joliffe, N.: *Dea Brigantia*. Archaeological Journal 98 (1941), 36-61.
Jones, David: *Epoch and Artist*. Faber, London, 1959.
Jones, Francis: *The Holy Wells of Wales*. University of Wales Press, Cardiff, 1954.
Jones, G., and Jones, T.: *The Mabinogion*. Dent, London, 1948.
Jones, Kelvin I. (ed.): *Strange Cornish Customs*. Oakmagic Publications, Penzance, 1997.
Jones, O. et. al. (ed.): *The Myrvyrian Archaiology of Wales*. Denbigh, 1870.
Jones, Prudence, & Pennick, Nigel: *A History of Pagan Europe*. Routledge, London, 1995.
Joyce, P.W.: *A Social History of Ancient Ireland*. Longmans, London, 1913.
Judge, Roy: *The Jack in the Green: A May Day Custom*. D.S. Brewer, Cambridge, 1977.
Jung, Carl Gustav: *Man and His Symbols*. Aldus, London, 1964.

Jung, Carl Gustav: *The Archetypes and the Collective Unconscious*. Routledge and Kegan Paul, London, 1971.
Kaul, Flemming; Marazov, Ivan; Best, Jan, and De Vries, Nanny: *Thracian Tales on the Gundestrup Cauldron*. Najade Press, Amsterdam, 1991.
Keiller, Alexander: *Windmill Hill and Avebury Excavations*, 1925-1939. Oxford University Press, Oxford, 1965.
Kennedy, P.: *Legendary Fictions of the Irish Celts*. London, 1891.
Kennedy, Peter (ed.): *Folksongs of Britain and Ireland*. Oak Publications, London/New York/Sydney/Cologne, 1984.
Keverne, Richard: *Tales of Old Inns*. Collins, London, 1955.
King, John: *The Celtic Druids' Year*. Blandford, London, 1994.
Kinsella, Thomas (trans.): *The Téin*. University of Philadelphia Press, Philadelphia, 1985.
Knott, E.: *Togail Bruidne Da Derga*. Dublin, 1936.
Lainé-Kerjean, C.: 'Le Calendrier Celtique'. Zeitschrift für celtische Philologie, XXIII. 1943.
Laing, Lloyd: *The Archaeology of Late Celtic Britain and Ireland c 400 - 1200 AD*. Methuen, London, 1975.
Lambert, Margaret, & Marx, Enid: *English Popular Art*. Merlin Press, London, 1989.
Larwood, Jacob, & Hotten, John Camden (1866): *English Inn Signs*. Chatto & Windus, London, 1951.
Leather, Ella Mary: *The Folk-lore of Herefordshire*. Jakeman & Carver, Hereford; Sidgwick & Jackson, London, 1912.
Le Braz, Anatole: *La Légende de la Mort*. Paris, 1893.
Le Braz, Anatole: *The Land of Pardons*. Methuen, London, 1906.
Ledwich, Dr.: *The Antiquities of Ireland*. Dublin, 1792.
Le Goff, Jacques: *The Medieval Imagination*. University of Chicago Press, Chicago & London, 1988.
Lehmacher, G.: 'The Ancient Celtic Year'. Journal of Celtic Studies, I, (1949-50).
Lengyel, Lancelot: *Le Secret des Celtes*. Robert Morel, Paris, 1969.
Leslie, S.: *St Patrick's Purgatory*. London, 1932.
*Liber Hymnorum*, ed. Henry Bradshaw Society. London, 1897.
Lightfoot, John: *Flora Scotica*. Edinburgh, 1772.
Little, George A.: *Dublin Before the Vikings*. M.H. Gill and Son, Dublin, 1957.
Lorenzoni, Piero: *English Eroticism*. Omega, Ware, 1984.
Luzel, F.M. (trans. Bryce, D.): *Celtic Folk-Tales from Armorica*. Llanerch, Lampeter, 1985.
Macalister, R. A. S.: *Studies in Irish Epigraphy*. 3 vols. Cambridge University Press, London, 1897, 1902, 1907.
Macalister, R. A. S.: *The Archeology of Ireland*. Methuen, London, 1928.
Macalister, R. A. S.: *The Secret Languages of Ireland*. Cambridge University Press, London, 1937.

Macalister, R. A. S. (ed. and trans.): *Lebor Gabála Erenn*. 4 vols. Irish Texts Society, Dublin, 1938-1956.
Macalister, R. A. S.: *Corpus Inscriptionum Insularum Celticarum*. Irish Texts Society. Dublin, 1945.
MacCana, Proinsias: *Celtic Mythology*. Hamlyn, London, 1970.
MacCrossan, Tadhg: *The Sacred Cauldron. Secrets of the Druids*. Llewellyn, St Paul, 1991.
MacCulloch, John Arnott: *The Religion of the Ancient Celts*. Constable, London, 1991.
Macleod, Fiona: *'Sea Magic and Running Water'*. Occult Review. London, 1902.
MacManus, Dermot: *The Middle Kingdom*. Colin Smythe, Gerrard's Cross, 1959.
MacNeill, E.: *Early Irish Laws and Institutions*. Dublin, n.d.
MacNeill, M.: *The Festival of Lughnasa*. Oxford University Press, Oxford, 1962..
Macqueen, J.: *Maponus in Medieval Tradition*. Transactions of the Dumfries and Galloway Natural History and Antiquarian Society XXXI (1954), 43-57.
Maier, Bernhard (trans. Cyril Edwards): *Dictionary of Celtic Religion and Culture*. Boydell, Woodbridge, 1994.
Mâle, Emil: *Le Fin du paganisme en* Gaul. Paris, 1950.
Matthews, J: *Taliesin*. Aquarian, London, 1991.
Matthews, J, & Stewart, R. J.: *Warriors of Arthur*. Blandford, London, 1987.
McNeill, F. Marian: *The Silver Bough*. Canongate, Edinburgh, 1989.
Merne, John: *A Handbook of Celtic Ornament*. Mercier Educational, Dublin, 1974.
Meyer, K. (ed. & trans.): *The Triads of Ireland*. Dublin, 1906.
Meyer, K.: *'The Expulsion of the Déssi'*. Y Cymmrodor XIV.
Milton, Roger: *The English Ceremonial Book. A History of Robes, Insignia and Ceremonies still in use in England*. David & Charles, Newton Abbot, 1972.
Monson-Fitzjohn, G.J.: *Quaint Signs of Olde Inns*. Herbert Jenkins, London, 1926.
Murphy, Gerard: *Early Irish Lyrics, 8th - 12th century*. Clarendon Press, Oxford, 1956.
Murray, Colin: *Ogham Divination Card Game*. Golden Section Order, London, 1977.
Murray, Colin: *'The Trees of the Forest', & 'Ogham Chart'*. Newsletter of the Golden Section Order, The Bardic Chair of Caer Llyndain, August 1979.
Murray, Liz, & Murray, Colin (artwork by Vanessa Card): *The Celtic Tree Oracle*. Rider, London, 1988.
Naddair, Kaledon (artwork by Edwin O'Donnelly et. al.): *Koelbren Cards I*. Inner Keltia, Edinburgh, 1984.
Naddair, Kaledon (artwork by Lorraine & Linda): *Koelbren Cards II*. Inner Keltia, Edinburgh, 1986.

Napier, A. David: *Masks, Transformation and Paradox*. Thames and Hudson, London, 1986.
Nash-Williams, V.E.: *The Early Christian Monuments of Wales*. University of Wales Press, Cardiff, 1950.
Newark, Tim: *Celtic Warriors 400 BC - AD 1600*. Blandford, London, 1988.
Nichols, J.: *The Progresses, Processions and Magnificent Festivities of King James the First*. London, 1828.
Nichols, Ross: *The Book of Druidry*. Aquarian, London, 1990.
Nicoll, A.: *Masks, Mimes and Miracles*. London, 1931.
Nilsson, M. P.: *Primitive Time Reckoning*. Cambridge, 1920.
O'Boyle, Seán: *Ogham, The Poet's Secret*. Gilbert Dalton, Dublin, 1980.
O'Curry, Eugene: *On the Manners and Customs of the Ancient Irish*. London, 1873.
O'Connell, Sir John: *The Honan Hostel Chapel, Cork*. Cork, 1916.
O'Donovan, J. (ed.): *The Book of Rights*. Dublin, 1847.
O'Donovan, J. (ed.): *Annals of the Kingdom of Ireland*. Dublin, 1856.
O'Donovan, J. (trans.), & Stokes, W. (ed.): *Cormac's Glossary*. Calcutta, 1868.
O'Grady, Standish H. (ed. & trans.): *Silva Gadelica*. London, 1892.
O'Hehir, Brendan: *The Origin, Development and History of the Ogham Script: Facts and Conjecture*. In *Exploring Rock Art* (transcribed and edited by Donald L. Cyr), Stonehenge Viewpoint, Sata Barbara, 1989.
Ó hOgáin, Dáithi: *Myth. Legend and Romance: An Encyclopedia of the Irish Folk Tradition*. Ryan, London, 1981.
O'Flaherty, Roderick: *Ogygia*. Dublin, 1793.
O'Kelleher, A., & Schoepperle, G. (ed. & trans.): *Betha Collum*. Chille. Urbana, 1918.
O'Murnaghan, Art: *The Book of Resurrection*. Ms. The National Museum of Ireland, Dublin (1922).
O'Rahilly, T.F.: *Early Irish History and Mythology*. Institute For Advanced Studies, Dublin, 1946.
O'Tuathaigh, Gearoid: *Ireland Before the Famine*. Dublin, 1972.
Owen, Trefor M.: *Welsh Folk Customs*. Gomer, Llandysul, 1987.
Owen, Trefor M.: *The Customs and Traditions of Wales*. University of Wales Press, Cardiff, 1991.
Painter, K.S.: *The Mildenhall Treasure*. British Museum, London, 1977.
Palmer, Roy: *The Folklore of Hereford & Worcester*. Logaston Press, Woonton Almeley, 1992.
Patch, H.R.: *The Otherworld*. Harvard University Press, Cambridge (Mass.), 1950.
Pegg, Bob: *Rites and Riots: Folk Customs of Britain and Europe*. Blandford, London, 1981.
Pennick, Nigel: *Ogham and Runic: Magical Writing of Old Britain and Northern Europe*. Fenris-Wolf, Bar Hill, 1978.
Pennick, Nigel: *Games of the Gods*. Rider, London, 1988.

Pennick, Nigel: *The Origin of Ogam and Runestaves.* In *Celtic Secrets* (ed. Donald L. Cyr). Stonehenge Viewpoint, Santa Barbara, 1990.
Pennick, Nigel: *Celtic Art in the Northern Tradition.* Nideck, Bar Hill, 1992.
Pennick, Nigel: *Anima Loci.* Nideck, Bar Hill, 1993.
Pennick, Nigel: *Practical Magic in the Northern Tradition.* Thoth, Loughborough, 1994.
Pennick, Nigel: *Secrets of East Anglian Magic.* Robert Hale, London, 1995.
Pennick, Nigel: *Secret Signs, Symbols and Sigils.* Capall Bann, Chieveley, 1996.
Pennick, Nigel: *Celtic Sacred Landscapes.* Thames and Hudson, London, 1996.
Pennick, Nigel: *The Inner Mysteries of the Goths.* Capall Bann, Chieveley, 1996.
Pennick, Nigel: *The Celtic Saints.* Thorsons, London, 1997.
Pennick, Nigel: *The Sacred World of the Celts.* Thorsons, London, 1997.
Pennick, Nigel: *The Celtic Cross.* Blandford, London, 1997.
Pennick, Nigel: *Crossing the Borderlines. Guising, Masking and Ritual Animal Disguises in the European Tradition.* Capall Bann, Chieveley, 1998.
Pennick, Nigel: *The Complete Illustrated Guide to Runes.* Element, Shaftesbury, 1999.
Pennick, Nigel, & Field, Helen: *The Goddess Year.* Capall Bann, Chieveley, 1996.
Pennick, Nigel, & Field, Helen: *The God Year.* Capall Bann, Chieveley, 1998.
Pennick, Nigel, & Jackson, Nigel: *The Celtic Oracle. The Ancient Art of the Druids.* Thorsons, London, 1992.
Peter, Thurstan (1912): *The Cornish Obby Oss.* Oakmagic Publications, Penzance, 1997.
Pittaway, Andy, & Scofield, Bernard: *The Complete Country Bizarre.* Astragal Books, London, 1976.
Planck, Dieter; Biel, Jörg; Süsskind, Gabriele, & Wais, André (eds.): *Der Keltenfürst von Hochdorf.* Landesdenkmalamt Baden-Württemberg, Thiess, Stuttgart, 1985.
Plenydd: *The Welsh Bardic Alphabet.* The Library of the European Tradition, Bar Hill, 1999.
Pokorny, J: Keltologie. Bern, 1935.
Portal, F.: *Des couleurs symboliques.* Paris, 1837.
Porteous, Alexander: *Forest Folklore.* George Allen & Unwin, London, 1928.
Pughe, John (trans.), and Ab Ithel, John Williams (ed.): *The Physicians of Myddvai: Maddygon Myddfai, or the Medical Practice of the celebrated Rhiwallon and his sons, of Myddvai, in Carmarthenshire, Physicians to Rhys Gryg, Lord of Dynevor and Ystrad Towy, About the Middle of the Thirteenth Century.* The Welsh Manuscript Society, Llandovery 1865..
Redknap, Mark: *The Christian Celts. Treasure of Late Celtic Wales.* National Museum of Wales, Cardiff, 1991.

Rees, Alwyn, & Rees, Brinley: *Celtic Heritage*. Thames and Hudson, London, 1967.
Rhys, John: *Celtic Folklore*. Oxford University Press, Oxford, 1901.
Rich, Barnaby: *The Description of Ireland*. London, 1610.
Richardson, L.J.D.: *The Word 'Ogham'*. Hodges, Figgis & Co.,Dublin, 1949.
Ross, Anne: *Pagan Celtic Britain*. Cardinal, London, 1967.
Ross, Anne: *The Folklore of the Scottish Highlands*. Batsford, London, 1976.
Ross, Anne: *The Pagan Celts*. Batsford, London, 1986.
Ross, Anne: *Druids, Gods and Heroes of Celtic Mythology*. Routledge & Kegan Paul, London, 1986.
Scott, M.: *Irish Folk and Fairy Tales*. (2 vols.). Sphere, London, 1983.
Seabac, An (ed.): *Triocha-céad Corca Dhuibne*. Dublin, 1893.
Seignolle, Claude: *Le Folklore de la Provence*. Paris, 1963.
Sharkey, John (ed.): *Ogham Monuments in Wales*. Texts by R. Rolt Brash and J. Romilly Allen. Llanerch, Felinfach, 1992.
Sheehy, Jeanne: *The Rediscovery of Ireland's Past. The Celtic Revival, 1830 - 1930*. Thames and Hudson, London, 1980.
Sills-Fuchs, Martha: *Der Mittagshirsch: die Wiederentdeckung des Keltischen Kalenders*. Edition S, Vienna, 1990.
Simpson, Jacqueline: *European Mythology*. Hamlyn, London, 1987.
Sjoestedt, Marie-Louise: *Gods and Heroes of the Celts*. University of California Press, Berkeley, 1982.
Spence, Lewis: *The Mysteries of Britain*. Rider, London, 1928.
Spence, Lewis: *The Magic Arts in Celtic Britain*. Aquarian, London, 1970.
Stewart, R. J.: *The Prophetic Vision of Merlin*. Arkana, London, 1986.
Stokes, W.: *'The Rennes Dindshenchas'*. Revue Celtique XVI (1895).
Stokes, W.: *'Bruiden Da Choca'*. Revue Celtique XXI (1900).
Strutt, Joseph (ed. Hone, William): *The Sports and Pastimes of the People of England*. London, 1830.
Tabor, Raymond: *Traditional Woodland Crafts*. Batsford, London, 1994.
Tiddy, R.J. E..: *The Mummer's Play*. Oxford University Press, Oxford, 1923.
Thurneysen, R.: *Die irische Helden- und Königssage*. Haale-Saale, 1921.
Tolkien, J.R.R.: *Tree and Leaf*. George Allen and Unwin, London, 1964.
Toynbee, J.M.C.: *Art In Roman Britain*. Thames and Hudson, London, 1962.
Varagnac, A.: *Civilisation traditionelle et genres de vie*. Paris, 1948.
Vendryes, J.: *'L'écriture ogamique et ses origines'*. Études Celtiques IV, 83-116.
Wade-Evans, A.W.: *Vitae Sanctorum Britanniae et Genealogiae*. University of Wales Press, Cardiff, 1944.
Waterhouse, George: *Antique Irish Brooches*. Dublin, 1872.
Webster, G.: *The British Celts and their Gods Under Rome*. London: Batsford, London, 1986.
White, G. Pawley (Gunwyn):*A Handbook of Cornish Surnames*. Privately Published, Camborne, 1972.
Wickham, Glynne: *Early English Stages 1300 to 1660. Volume One 1300 to 1576*. Routledge & Kegan Paul, London, 1966.

Wilde, Lady: *Ancient Legends, Mystic Charms and Superstitions of Ireland.* London, 1887.
Williams, G.J.: *'William Robert o'r Ydwal'.* Llán Cymru, III (1954-55), 48 - 50.
Williams, G.J.: *'Iolo Morganwg'.* Cardiff, 1956.
Williams, G.J.: *'Glamorgan Customs in the 18th Century'.* Gwerin I (1957).
Williams, G.J., & Jones E.J. (eds.): *Gramadegau'r Perceirddiaid.* Cardiff, 1934.
Williams, I, & Roberts, T. (eds.): *Cywyddau Dafydd ap Gwilym a'i Gyfoeswr.* University of Wales Press, Cardiff, 1935.
Williams, I, & Williams, J. Ll. (eds.): *Gwaith Guto'r Glyn.* University of Wales Press, Cardiff, 1939.
Wilson, Steve: Robin Hood: *The Spirit of the Forest.* Neptune Press, London, 1993.
Wimberley, L.C.: *Folklore of the English and Scottish Ballads.* Frederick Unger, New York, 1928.
Wirth, Hermann: *Die Heilige Urschrift der Menschheit.* Köhler und Amerlang, Leipzig, 1934.
Woll, Johanna: *Alte Festbräuche im Jahreslauf.* Eugen Ulmer, Stuttgart, 1991.
Wood-Martin, W.G.: *Pagan Ireland.* London, 1895.
Wood-Martin, W.G.: *Traces of the Elder Faiths of Ireland.* London, 1902.
Woods, K.S.: *Rural Crafts of England.* Harrap, London, 1949.
Wright, Dudley: *Druidism: The Ancient Faith of Britain.* London, 1924.
Wright, Philip A.: *Old Farm Implements.* David & Charles, Newton Abbot, 1974.
York, Michael: *The Divine Versus the Asurian. An Interpretation of Indo-European Cult and Myth.* International Scholars Publications, Bethesda (Maryland), 1995.

# Index

Adder in the Heath, 72
Aibítir, 27, 31, 61, 78-79, 81, 144, 149, 153
Alba, 6, 39, 58, 149
Alder, 21, 32, 36-39, 78-79, 82, 135, 157, 159
Alternative Correspondences, 69
Alternative Numbers and Orders, 69
An Ogam Craobh, 28-29, 31, 33
Andraste, 83
Apple of Aillinn, 18
Arms Ogham, 74
Ash, 20-21, 40, 60, 79, 85, 111, 133, 150, 152, 154, 157, 159
Aspen, 21, 51, 60, 62, 78, 155, 158-159
Auraicept na néces, 1, 11, 15, 17, 20, 27, 33, 43, 48, 159, 176
Awen, 20, 80, 130-131, 133-134, 149

Bardic Frames, 140
Biere Stones, 77-78
Birch, 15, 20-21, 33-35, 39, 78-79, 87, 108-112, 115, 150, 156-157, 159, 163
Birchen Maypoles, 109
Black Wood of Rannoch, 89
Blackthorn, 20-21, 56, 92, 116, 151, 153, 158-159
Bonded Ogham, 71
Book of Ballymote, 1, 11, 13, 15, 18-19, 23, 27-28, 32-35, 38, 40-41, 46, 51, 53, 55, 58, 60, 62-65, 68-72, 75, 79, 159
Book of Leinster, 16-17, 175

Book of St Albans, 51
Branch Ogham, 27
Breass MacElathan, 13
Brehon Laws, 18, 40, 61
Bressay Stone, 29
Brocéliande, 89
Broom, 20-21, 55, 59, 111-114, 159-160
Burmanus, 83

Callirius, 82
Ceart Ogam, 32
Coir Ogham, 74-75
Colin Murray, 0, 9, 24, 28, 58, 60, 62-63, 125, 144
Colour Ogham, 24, 75
Con Ogham, 74
Council of Arles, 91
Crab Apple, 51-52
crane-skin 'medicine bag', 64
Cuchulaínn, 17
Cypress, 21, 46

Deus Fagus, 82
Din Ogam, 27
Dog Ogham, 74
Droim, 15, 22, 28-29, 151

Ebillion, 141, 143, 151
Elder, 21, 46, 56-57, 61, 64, 122, 156, 158-159, 185
Elm, 20, 34, 43, 58-59, 78-79, 81, 121, 153, 158-159
En Ogam, 27

Faun Ogham, 73
Fercetne, 19

Fionn MacCumhaill, 51
Fionn's Oghams, 73
Fleasc Filidh, 17, 152
Forêt de Huelgoat, 89

Gaels, 6, 83
Golden Section Order, 9, 24-25, 28, 60, 63-64, 181
Gooseberry, 21, 64, 156, 158
Gorse, 59, 159-160
Grape, 52
Green Man, 3, 97-99, 101, 103, 105, 107

Hawthorn, 41, 43, 116, 152, 156-157
Hazel, 20-21, 48-49, 51, 65, 67, 78, 83, 111, 133, 140, 150-152, 156-157, 159
Heather, 60, 79, 111, 150, 152, 158-160
Hill Ogham, 27
Holly, 46-48, 51, 81, 92, 150-151, 157, 159
holy well of St Fintan, 119
Honeysuckle, 21, 63, 158
Human Ogham, 74

Iolo Morganwg, 125, 127, 185
Ivy, 20-21, 47, 53, 55, 60, 79, 151, 158-159, 164

Jack-in-the-Green, 103, 105, 107

Kiln Tree, 33-34, 40-41
Kvistrunar, 32, 153

Leabhar na hUidhré, 16-17
Lebor Gabála Erenn, 19, 181
Lindisfarne Gospels, 73
Little Devil Doubt, 113
Llewellyn Sion, 127-128, 131, 139

Medionemeton, 83
Merlin, 87-88, 92-95, 97, 101, 104, 180, 184, 188
Merry Order of St Bridget, 115

Nemesis, 83
Nemetona, 83

Oak, 9, 20-21, 43, 45-46, 78, 85, 88, 91-93, 95, 97, 101-103, 108, 122, 141, 151, 157, 159, 163, 178, 180
Ogam Inarbach, 28
Ogham 'Point Towards the Pit', 71
Ogham Adlen Fid, 72
Ogham Airenach, 72
Ogham Consaine, 68
Ogham Craobh, 22, 27, 33, 51, 59, 64, 69, 73, 147, 149
Ogham Deginach, 72
Ogham Feadha, 0, 8-9, 11, 27, 65, 77, 79, 162
Ogham of 'Fionn's Window', 73
Ogham of Banishment, 28
Ogham of Consonants, 68
Ogham of Extraordinary Disturbance, 72
Ogham of the Foreigner, 71
Ogham of the Multitudes, 71
Ogham Pin, 9
Ogham Terminology, 15, 28
Ogma Cermait, 13
Ogma Grian Aineach, 11, 13
Ogmios, 13

Palm Coelbren, 143
Palm, 58, 143-144
Peithenyn, 141-143, 155
Picts, 7
Piercing Ogham, 72
Race of Crimthann, 6
Reed, 21, 53, 55, 152, 158

**187**

rhabdomancy, 35, 155
Righ Ogam, 27
Right Ogham, 32
Rigonemetis, 83
Robert Graves, 9, 24, 39, 58, 147, 162
Rowan, 34-35, 37, 46, 51, 78, 82, 111, 133, 140, 150-151, 157, 159

Scholastic Ogham, 9-10, 29
Scholastic Oghams, 8, 29
Schwäbish-Allemannisch Fasnacht, 16
Scots Pine, 65
Silver Fir, 58
Sluag Ogham, 71
Snaiti Snimach, 28
Spindle Tree, 62
Sron Ogham, 75
St Colum Cille, 92
Staves of the Poets, 17, 156
Swine Ogham, 75

Tabhall Lorga, 17, 156
Tables of the Poets, 17, 156
Tablet Staves, 17
Taeb Ogham Tlachtga, 28
Taibhli Fileadh, 17, 156
Tain Bó Cúalnge, 11, 17
Tamlorga Filidh, 17, 156
The Final Ogham, 64, 72
The Side Ogham of Tlachtga, 28
The Twining, 28

Unison Ogham, 71
Uraicecht na n Eiges, 11
Vernemeton, 83

Wand of the Poet, 17
Wall-Fern Ogham, 72
Wearyall Hill, 117

White Willow, 39
Wild Men, 99-101, 103, 105, 107
Windmill Hill stones, 5
Witch Hazel, 21, 65, 67
Wood of Caledon, 89, 101, 154
Woodwose, 99, 104
Wren Boys' Song, 45

Yew, 18, 21, 38, 61-62, 78-79, 92, 153, 158-159

# FREE DETAILED CATALOGUE

Capall Bann is owned and run by people actively involved in many of the areas in which we publish. A detailed illustrated catalogue is available on request, SAE or International Postal Coupon appreciated. **Titles can be ordered direct from Capall Bann, post free in the UK** (cheque or PO with order) or from good bookshops and specialist outlets.

Do contact us for details on the latest releases at: **Capall Bann Publishing, Freshfields, Chieveley, Berks, RG20 8TF.** Titles include:

A Breath Behind Time, Terri Hector
Angels and Goddesses - Celtic Christianity & Paganism, M. Howard
Asyniur - Womens Mysteries in the Northern Tradition, S McGrath
Beginnings - Geomancy, Builder's Rites & Electional Astrology in the European Tradition, Nigel Pennick
Between Earth and Sky, Julia Day
Book of the Veil , Peter Paddon
Caer Sidhe - Celtic Astrology and Astronomy, Vol 1, Michael Bayley
Call of the Horned Piper, Nigel Jackson
Celtic Faery Shamanism, Catrin James
Celtic Lore & Druidic Ritual, Rhiannon Ryall
Celtic Sacrifice - Pre Christian Ritual & Religion, Marion Pearce
Celtic Saints and the Glastonbury Zodiac, Mary Caine
Compleat Vampyre - The Vampyre Shaman, Nigel Jackson
Creating Form From the Mist - The Wisdom of Women in Celtic Myth and Culture, Lynne Sinclair-Wood
Crystal Doorways, Simon & Sue Lilly
Crossing the Borderlines - Guising, Masking & Ritual Animal Disguise in the European Tradition, Nigel Pennick
Dragons of the West, Nigel Pennick
Earth Harmony - Places of Power, Holiness & Healing, Nigel Pennick
Earth Magic, Margaret McArthur
Eildon Tree (The) Romany Language & Lore, Michael Hoadley
Enchanted Forest - The Magical Lore of Trees, Yvonne Aburrow
Fairies in the Irish Tradition, Molly Gowen
Familiars - Animal Powers of Britain, Anna Franklin
Forest Paths - Tree Divination, Brian Harrison, Ill. S. Rouse
From Past to Future Life, Dr Roger Webber
God Year, The, Nigel Pennick & Helen Field
Goddess on the Cross, Dr George Young
Goddess Year, The, Nigel Pennick & Helen Field

Handbook For Pagan Healers, Liz Joan
Healing Stones, Sue Philips
Herb Craft - Shamanic & Ritual Use of Herbs, Lavender & Franklin
In Search of Herne the Hunter, Eric Fitch
Inner Mysteries of the Goths, Nigel Pennick
Legend of Robin Hood, The, Richard Rutherford-Moore
Lid Off the Cauldron, Patricia Crowther
Light From the Shadows - Modern Traditional Witchcraft, Gwyn
Living Tarot, Ann Walker
Lost Lands & Sunken Cities (2nd ed.), Nigel Pennick
Magical Guardians - Exploring the Spirit and Nature of Trees, Philip Heselton
Magick Without Peers, Ariadne Rainbird & David Rankine
Masks of Misrule - Horned God & His Cult in Europe, Nigel Jackson
Mirrors of Magic - Evoking the Spirit of the Dewponds, P Heselton
Mysteries of the Runes, Michael Howard
New Celtic Oracle The, Nigel Pennick & Nigel Jackson
Oracle of Geomancy, Nigel Pennick
Patchwork of Magic - Living in a Pagan World, Julia Day
Pillars of Tubal Cain, Nigel Jackson
Psychic Self Defence - Real Solutions, Jan Brodie
Real Fairies, David Tame
Runic Astrology, Nigel Pennick
Sacred Animals, Gordon MacLellan
Sacred Celtic Animals, Marion Davies, Ill. Simon Rouse
Sacred Grove - The Mysteries of the Forest, Yvonne Aburrow
Sacred Geometry, Nigel Pennick
Sacred Ring - Pagan Origins of British Folk Festivals, M. Howard
Secret Places of the Goddess, Philip Heselton
Secret Signs & Sigils, Nigel Pennick
Stony Gaze, Investigating Celtic Heads John Billingsley
Subterranean Kingdom, The, revised 2nd ed, Nigel Pennick
Tree: Essence of Healing, Simon & Sue Lilly
Tree: Essence, Spirit & Teacher, Simon & Sue Lilly
Wildwitch - The Craft of the Natural Psychic, Poppy Palin
Wildwood King, Philip Kane

# FREE detailed catalogue and FREE 'Inspiration' magazine
Contact: Capall Bann Publishing, Freshfields, Chieveley, Berks, RG20 8TF